Enlarge Your World

JOHN WARREN STEEN

BROADMAN PRESS
Nashville, Tennessee

Some of the material used in this book has appeared in a slightly different form in *Sunday School Senior Adults* and in *Mature Living*. Used by permission. Unless otherwise noted, all Scripture quotations are taken from the King James Version of the Bible.

Dewey Decimal Classification: 248.85

Subject headings: CHRISTIAN LIFE//ELDERLY

Library of Congress Catalog Card Number: 77–090218

Printed in the United States of America

Contents

To my son

John Warren Steen, III

who bears a similar name

and a similar love for older people

Introduction

Years ago I saw the Ronald Colman movie *Lost Horizon.* I recall the shock I felt as the young girl left Shangri-la and developed hundreds of wrinkles in her pretty face. The aging process in that movie, although a thrill for the makeup artist, was a tragedy that separated the two lovers.

But the insightful part of the story was not so much the sudden aging as it was the punishment that comes from refusing to age naturally. The girl had put off aging, and it came to her with the devastating force of a tornado, sweeping her away from the person she loved.

You need to treat the process of aging with respect. You may cover up some of its evidence for a while with face lifts and hair transplants—but inevitably age will demonstrate its power. I say that it's better to recognize it, befriend it, and let it enrich your life.

My Interest in Aging

I've always been fascinated with older people. My grandmothers used to hold me on their laps. I liked that. Grandmother Steen would rock me to sleep. Not Grandmother Henry—she told me ghost stories and scared the sleep out of me. And we stayed up late by her hearth, eating her marvelous tea cakes and fried apple pies.

My grandfather, who later lived in our home, used to read his Bible every day. He used to tell me some of the facts he had rediscovered. Although I didn't agree with all he said, I enjoyed hearing his views. I have always liked being around older people.

My interest in aging developed with my schooling. When I was a seminary student working as a summer assistant to Herbert Gabhart, pastor of First Baptist Church, Williamsburg, Kentucky, he challenged me to write a sermon on aging, entitled, "Pardon Me, Your Age Is Showing." He also advised me when I went to a new church to get to know the shut-ins first of all.

I followed his advice. I wrote that sermon and worked out a philosophy of aging that I still believe is right. I learned to visit the shut-ins when I moved to a new pastorate and found them a blessing. They prayed for my work.

In one town, my first funeral to conduct was that of a suicide victim. The day before the service some of the people wondered if the new pastor could handle such a heavy responsibility as that kind of funeral. A black nurse with one of the shut-ins had met me when I went to call on the blind woman she helped. I prayed for them both, the woman and the nurse. That black woman said to one of the nervous, talkative women in that town, "Don't you worry. That new preacher is the Lord's man. The Lord's going to tell him what to do."

Her words spread over the town like fire through a field of dry sage. My pastoral role was established because of my visit to a ninety-year-old woman and her helper.

When I first heard of Golden Age Clubs back in the sixties, I was impressed. Since then, I have had the pleasure of compiling a list of senior adult church groups, visiting at least some of them, working with their leaders, and writing for them.

Senior adults have shown me by their participation in conferences and meetings that they want to have fun—but more than that, they want to enlarge their world. If I can help them, I will feel gratified.

My biggest temptation in working with the aging is to oversentimentalize them. I sometimes glamorize and romanticize them. I'll try to be careful in this book; but, at least, I have warned you.

I can laugh at age—my own or somebody else's. The only senior adults I will laugh at are those who want you to laugh along with them at the foibles of aging.

So let's have a feast. Welcome to the table. We're going to talk about what you can do to enlarge your world. Perhaps you'll like some of the ideas and not care for some of the others. If some of the ideas in this book can spark a new thought in your mind and fire up your energies, I'll feel that the adventure has been worthwhile.

Two Headlights

A minister of senior adults said to me, "We've done the easy things. We've been on tours and done crafts. Now the hard work begins—we want to study and to minister. Now we want to get involved with the world and its needs."

His words were similar to those of a distinguished senior

adult planner in Kansas City, Elbert Cole, who said, "We started with Meals on Wheels and service projects. Then we went on to Adventures in Learning and other educational projects, with which we reached even more people." Both emphases were important to Cole.

These two ideas—ministry and continuing education—are important to me. I consider them the two headlights that guide senior adult work into the dark and unknown future. These two ideas—ministry and education—will light up areas that have appeared dark for older people.

The world is ready to respond to people who know what they want and ask for it. Recently I heard the story of an Oklahoma millionaire who gave a large amount of money to interdenominational Oral Roberts University. Someone inquired, "Why didn't you give that money to Oklahoma Baptist University?"

He responded, "Because they didn't ask me."

Senior adult, I invite you to ask for what you want and to enlarge your world. I challenge you to affirm your maturity. You can make an impact on your world. If you don't know how, listen to the ideas I have compiled from working with and reading about senior adults.

I'm not a senior adult yet, but I'm nearer that category than I am the teenage one. Sure, I'm growing older. I'm fifty-two and grateful for these years God has given me. As I think about my future, I want to become more effective in speaking out for and with senior adults. I invite you to grow bold along with me.

1
Grow Bold Along with Me

Sure, I said bold. I mean bold. If I had meant Walter Mitty timidity, I would have said it. Grow bold, and you'll find power.

Senior adults, made in God's image, should share in his power and his glory. He wants them to. But some have been afraid.

People wonder, *Is power wrong?* Not if it's used in the right way. Of course, a river, instead of providing hydroelectric energy, can escape its banks in a fit of wild destruction. But properly harnessed, the water can light homes and turn factory wheels. Senior adult power can be used correctly and profitably.

Unfortunately, too many people in society have implied or even said, "OK, old timer, sit over there out of my sight." They have designated the older person a parasite—living off the nourishment of youth. That's garbage. Don't pay any attention to such stupidity.

Why have older Christians generated so little power? Why have they made so little impact on public life? I asked a group of senior adults. One man said, "We feel powerless because we feel that one little voice won't count."

Another said, "We are just plain lazy."

A woman said, "We haven't set the example for young people we should have. Maybe it's because we haven't had an example set for us."

Another reason they implied but never enunciated was this: Something about activism seems evil, and dedicated Christians will separate themselves from it.

Still another reason is the cultural straitjacket that older people are expected to wear. Younger people have expected restraint from their elders. Instead of asking them to be advisers and guides, as in other cultures, modern America has wanted its elders to keep a low profile.

Younger citizens have wanted to make babies out of senior citizens. A friend in his seventies, Hank, told me about buying a Christmas tree. Even though the balsam tree was a small one, the girl who sold it insisted on taking it from the lot out to Hank's car. He was amused that she thought of him as too old and weak to carry a little Christmas tree.

Younger people often underestimate senior adult interests and activities. A young surgeon told me he was amazed at how often people in their seventies asked him, "How soon after surgery can I resume sexual activities?" His expectations hadn't been too high.

I say it's time for senior adults to carry Christmas trees, live their own life-style, climb up on soapboxes, and exert their power for God's glory. The world is ready for senior impact.

A materialistic society places value on one's productivity. Since the custom has been for a person to retire at sixty-five, the retiree was considered a nonproductive element—like a sucker on a tomato vine.

The winds of change are blowing. Culture is undergoing a change. The phenomenon of the graying of America is taking place.

Go back and rediscover the roots. Find what the Bible says about aging, and you'll discover a modern, up-to-date idea that the world hasn't quite grasped yet. Look at the word *elder*, and you'll find it rubbed with honor—giving off a glow of respect. Ancient Hebrews cherished the leadership skills and accumulated wisdom of the elder. Moses depended on elders for help.

Early Christians didn't abandon the word (even though Jesus had criticized a dependence on the traditions of the elders). Church members called their leaders by the customary term, *elder*. The New Testament draws a picture of older people as special ministers in God's service. To these Christian senior adults, much has been given by God; and from them much is required.

Note the qualities of life and special ministries of older men and older women spelled out in Titus 2:1–5. Compare these verses with the instructions to widows and elders in 1 Timothy 5:1–25. The biblical emphasis on wisdom, honor, and continuing service needs to continue today.

Learning from Nonagenarians

Let me reveal a quirk of mine: I'm fascinated by nonagenarians. If my friend Mr. Crossway told me to stick my head in a bucket of tar, I'd probably do it. If Mrs. Perry said she'd meet me at a haunted house in Franklin, Tennessee, I'd be there at the appointed time.

What are nonagenarians? People who have lived to

be ninety to ninety-nine years of age. I admire their tenacity. They've hung on to life like a bulldog hanging on to a prowler's britches.

Do you know many people in their nineties? I know lots of these nonagenarians. I think of Dr. Hastings, a retired preacher who writes poems reminiscent of John Milton. Or Mrs. Wilder, who brightened the home of her son-in-law, Howard Colson, until recently when she chose to return to her home state of South Carolina to enter a retirement home. Or the lady from Meridian, Mississippi, who came to the Senior Adult Chautauqua at Ridgecrest in the minivan that belongs to the First Baptist Church. Or the man from Jackson, Tennessee, whom I met touring Mammoth Cave with his church group.

My wife's grandfather, John Roeder, although dead now, lives on in my memories as one who in his nineties continued to carve walking canes and fans out of wood and to hunt squirrels on his Kentucky farm. Also continuing in my memory is the ninety-five-year-old Richmond, Virginia, native who sang "How Great Thou Art" before a large audience at Ridgecrest.

Another ninety-year-old friend I've never seen in person is Christopher Black. He lives in a retirement village in Yukon, Oklahoma. I've corresponded with this man. I've been impressed with the way he loves to put his ideas in poems and distribute them to the other residents in his retirement complex. He visits each of the 150 residents about once a week.

He turned ninety on February 1, 1978. These were the words that he wrote for that occasion:

The time has come I've crossed the line,
Of passing to ninety from eighty-nine.
It's been a good life, interesting, too,
Four score and ten—now to live anew.
Those years were filled with various moods.
Of cares and grief of many kinds,
Through pleasant days and happy times,
In this life of mine, past eighty-nine.

If I could live my life anew
With kindness love and laughter,
To each I'd show greater feeling,
To God my trust ever after.
Make the life of each I met
More happy and content,
Until that day when I'm no longer here,
Knowing my life well spent.

—Christopher Black

I guess I know Daisy Perry best and admire her the most—she's ninety-three. She doesn't unload a lot of past history on you unless you ask for it. But I love to get her to talk about her ancestor on the Cherry side who fought with General Custer (and survived! You see, he was wounded the day before the Battle of Little Big Horn and didn't participate in it). She tells me about her father-in-law, Mr. Wait, who was a founding father of Wake Forest University. They named the handsome chapel on the new Winston-Salem campus for him. I sat in that Williamsburg-style edifice for my son's graduation from college, and I thought about Mrs. Perry and her father-in-law.

But Daisy Perry's not a relic from antiquity. Of course, she's firmly rooted in the past; but she's producing fruit in the present. She belongs to a church that has lots of youth—she knows them, and they love her. She encourages them. She makes anyone around her feel good.

Mrs. Perry is a connecting link with the past. When the editors of the *Broadman Hymnal* were seeking a wide representation in the 1952 edition of the hymnal, they asked her to recall some Moravian songs from her past in Winston-Salem, North Carolina. She spouted into a recorder the words to "Jesus Makes My Heart Rejoice." At ninety-three, she still remembers every word of that glorious hymn. It's like a credo for her. She depends on the strength and leadership that Jesus gives her. Imagine her twinkling eyes as she says these words:

> Jesus makes my heart rejoice,
>   I'm his sheep, and know his voice;
> He's a Shepherd, kind and gracious,
>   And his pastures are delicious;
> Constant love to me he shows,
>   Yea, my very name he knows.
>
> Trusting his mild staff always,
>   I go in and out in peace;
> He will feed me with the treasure
>   Of his grace in richest measure;
> When athirst to him I cry,
>   Living water he'll supply.
>
> Should not I for gladness leap,
>   Led by Jesus as his sheep?
> For when these blest days are over,
>   To the arms of my dear Savior
> I shall be conveyed to rest:
>   Amen, yea, my lot is blest.[1]

The famous French artist Marc Chagall, about the time he turned ninety, said, "You have to work while you're alive, because if you don't work you start to die." The creative man has lived by those words.

What common denominators describe these wonderful people who are now living in their tenth decade of life: a proper respect for the past without letting it overpower the present, an alertness to new friends, a willingness to get out and go even when in pain, a dependence on God for strength and guidance, and a desire to stay busy doing something constructive for other people.

These people are like the old apple tree that Longfellow pointed to. It's putting on a little new growth every year, he said. These nonagenarians are growing—they're maturing. They're beyond the age of childbearing, but they're still in the age of fruitbearing.

If the good Lord gives me the opportunity to live to be ninety, I have some good models to identify with. I want to be alert, growing, helpful to others, and trusting God for his daily mercies.

Expect Some Changes

More people than ever are collecting antiques, and those items are bringing in big prices at antique stores, auctions, and flea markets. The nostalgia craze has hit America like an epidemic. Foolish? No. Think of it this way. If people begin to treasure old washbowls and coatracks, if they think that weathered barns are beautiful—then they might begin to reevaluate older people. They might treasure old specimens of early Americana and put special value on anybody born in the last century.

Young adults might not concede that wrinkles are beautiful, but they might admit that wrinkles are badges of experience—proof that one has lived through six or eight decades of trying times—fighting a battle with poverty, with discouragement, and with health, all the while. So wear your wrinkles proudly—what would a road map be with no lines on the pages?

I know of one grandmother who took her little granddaughter shopping at a cosmetic counter. There the woman bought a skin cream that was guaranteed to remove wrinkles. After the woman tried it out for a few days, the child told her she should get her money back.

Another grandmother posed for her picture. Her grandson took a long time in painting it. She asked why it took him that long. He replied, "I want it to be perfect. I want to get in all the wrinkles."

Both grandmothers told these stories with pride. They weren't ashamed of their wrinkles or of their grandchildren's fascination with them. After all, the skin shows just one part of the aging process. But you can admit the wrinkles are there. Yes, you can wear them proudly.

January 1977 was a turning point—that's when *Roots* was shown on TV. That unique series of programs opened the eyes of Jane Doe and John Q. Public to the heritage and pride of Afro-Americans. Others have a pride in their past, too. Long before that showing, some individuals were turning to their state archives to trace their ancestry. Many more people seem interested now.

A young cousin of mine from California, a college boy, is interested in the Steen family and traveled back to Mississippi to find out about his ancestors.

A number of states are offering outdoor pageants that depict a rich cultural heritage. Churches are staging historical pageants and writing up histories as they've never done before. And the oral history has become a valuable technique for preserving the personal viewpoint of times past.

All of these movements have formed a tornadolike agitation that is producing a vortex of power. Senior adults can rejoice. They can cheer the results. Every time someone gets a true appreciation of the past, that person will likely appreciate an elder who has lived in the past and can convey some of its message to the present century.

The buying power of senior adults is increasing. With more older people better educated and better off financially than any past generation of elders, they have become the target of the capitalist. Gerber Foods, for instance, has dropped the slogan "Babies are our business, our only business." Now Gerber is selling insurance to elders.

Look for a change in the political scene. The latent power of the remote Victoria Falls, cascading in the middle of the African continent, is nothing compared with the latent power of senior adults here. When either power is fully channeled, it can bring about great changes for the good. Senior adults will form a larger and larger voting bloc in the next several years and into the next century. Politicans will look with respect on the aged and seek to get their votes.

All these indications of a changing culture will result in better conditions for the senior adults. More power is on the way. The political, social, and religious scenes are changing. The drama of senior adulthood is about to open on the Broadway of human understanding.

The Fascinating Process of Aging

Elapsed time photography has produced the miraculous scenes of a flower opening—from bud to flower in less than ten seconds. It has also demonstrated the hitherto unobserved process of a human fetus developing in a womb. Each of these events is a part of the fascinating process of aging.

A teenage girl and her grandmother were going to visit a museum. They found a sign at the entrance: "Senior Citizens Free." The girl was impressed and said, "It must be nice to be your age and get in free."

"It's wonderful, my dear." The older woman's answer was classic. "But there's a catch; even though you're old enough to get in free, you keep getting older."

The process keeps going on. It appears to strike only those who develop gray hair and wrinkles. But the miraculous process is happening to all. The wonder of it is that many young people think it will never happen to them.

A friend of mine with a beautiful English accent, Stuart Arnold, said that his little girl found a gray hair on his head one night and told him he was aging. "Not any faster than you are, my deah," he replied.

Everybody is aging. Sure, the process shows up on some people more than it does on others. But stop and think about the fact that *everybody* is growing older. This fact puts us in a great democracy of humanity. We are all equal—everybody is getting older.

The corollary of this fact is that anybody who criticizes another for aging is foolish. Persons who close their minds and stop learning are "old"—even at twenty. They deserve pity. A person with prejudice against the aging is shortsighted indeed—the person who criticizes, who ridicules the aging, will be in that same vulnerable position someday. Therefore, the wisest person is the advocate for the aged.

Advocacy is not just an altruistic activity. Persons who fight for the elderly are more than just do-gooders. Those persons are self-serving (in the best sense of the word). Advocates who demand better treatment for the aging are taking out insurance for the treatment they expect to receive when they get old. This motivation is prudent and self-affirming—not just unselfish and altruistic.

Frankly, I want to be an advocate for the aging as long as I live. I want to help others, but I also want for myself the rights and respect I feel I will deserve when I am older.

The Hymn Society of America conducted a contest and selected the ten best hymns about aging. Out of that ten, I thought one stood out. Here is that one, celebrating the idea of age (you can sing it to the tune of "Angels from the Realms of Glory"):

Come, Ye Elders, Those Engaging

Come, ye elders, those engaging
In the art of growing old;
Let us celebrate our aging,
Let our gratitude be told.

God, we praise thee; Lord, we thank thee,
For thy blessings manifold.

Loving friendships long enduring
Sweeten hours with gracious thought.

Others, with their tender caring,
Comfort, peace and joy have brought.

God, we praise thee; Lord, we thank thee;
For thy grace bestowed unsought.

Time we have, at last, for dreaming;
Time to study; time to grow;
Latent talents thus revealing,
Richer lives we learn to know.

God, we praise thee; Lord, we thank thee
For the gifts thou dost bestow.

Aging is a time for gladness;
Fear and doubts let us destroy;
Let no heart be filled with sadness;
Celebrate! Glad songs employ.

God, we praise thee; Lord, we thank thee.
Fill our hearts with love and joy! [2]

Getting a Factual View of Aging

With so much happening in the present, I'm like the egotistical athlete who said, "I can't wait to see what I'll be like tomorrow." I can't wait to see what senior adulthood will be like.

The picture most of us have of older persons is one we have formed from our own observations, from meeting people and talking eyeball to eyeball, and from listening to folktales and myths of aging. A more scientific way of finding out about older persons comes from research.

Many of the conclusions about older people were just hunches and guesses until 1974. At that time the National Council on the Aging, Inc., commissioned Louis Harris and Associates, Inc., to conduct a major, in-depth survey. The sample group consisted of 4,254 individuals. They represented a cross section of the public eighteen years of age and older.

Most of the answers in this project vary according to the age category of the respondent. For instance, when they were asked about the best years of life, people under forty indicated a time near their own age. But people over forty chose an earlier period. Both groups, however, were similar in their answer about the worst years of a person's life. About one-third of both age groups chose the sixties and seventies as the worst years.[3]

The main reason many of the respondents chose the older years as the worst ones is the bad health that is associated with those years.

Contrasting answers in the older and younger groups really shows up in a comparison of experienced problems with expected problems. In other words, the general public listed what they thought were serious problems for most people over sixty-five, and people over sixty-five listed what they actually found were serious problems for them. The biggest discrepancies occurred in the following areas: not enough job opportunities, loneliness, and not feeling needed. None was as bad as expected. Only three senior adults in ten think of loneliness as a serious problem. Only two out of ten consider not feeling needed as a serious problem. Only one out of ten finds a problem in not enough job opportunities.

Many people think that senior adults live in fear of being robbed or attacked on the street. In the sample, only 24 percent listed this as an important problem; but

46 percent of the general public thought it a problem.

One question on the Harris survey was this: What makes a person a useful member of the community? Older people felt that helping and serving others was important, along with being friendly and being a good neighbor. People under sixty-five had a different view. They put a larger stress on taking part in community activities and less stress on being friendly and being a good neighbor. A large number—79 percent of the senior adults—perceived themselves as useful or very useful members of their communities.

The Harris survey showed an interest in doing volunteer work but not a lot of participation. One shocking fact emerged: Having the time to work doesn't make a volunteer worker. A higher proportion of *employed* people sixty-five and older do volunteer work; older *nonemployed* volunteers account for only 20 percent of that group. The main activities that involved these volunteers included the following activities: health and mental health (work in a hospital or related organization)—23 percent, providing transportation for aged or handicapped—21 percent, voter registration and other civic affairs—17 percent, visiting and telephoning the homebound—17 percent, working in giveaway programs (clothes or food)—16 percent, and helping with family and child-care services—15 percent.

My own observations are similar to the survey findings. When I talk with older persons, I get the impression that they would like for their churches to point out ways in which they can express their Christian faith. They want to do something practical. Yet they don't know what.

They want to do more than just listen to an inspiring message from their pastor or Sunday School teacher.

These people remember the day many years ago when they made a profession of faith in Christ. After they walked down a church aisle, the preacher said to them, "Take a seat." Some have been sitting ever since. They're tired of a sedentary Christianity; they want some action. Guilty twinges make them know that they need some spiritual exercise.

In a recent survey made by the Sunday School Board, senior adults revealed details of their interest. They listed the top four volunteer job preferences in the following order: helping needy people in their community, prospect visitation, Sunday School teacher, and nursing home ministry. Then they listed four items that tied for the next place: children's worker, Church Training leader, music leader, and other places of service. They chose deacon last of all—perhaps because 58.7 percent of the respondents were women and didn't consider themselves eligible.

When the statisticians from the Sunday School Board asked the sample public which of nine ministries should be offered by the respondent's church, the answers were fascinating. Respondents ranked the activities in the following preferential order:

    weekday Bible study—30.8 percent
    weekday recreation—28.2 percent
    tape service for shut-ins—25.6 percent
    retreats—15.4 percent
    senior adult day—15.4 percent
    senior adult choir—12.8 percent

help with financial and emotional problems—11.5 percent

other weekday activities—11.5 percent

senior adult month—11.5 percent

On a question about volunteering for service, several people wrote in an additional response. One person would like to serve as a bus captain. Another would like to be a choir member. Another would be interested in church property maintenance. Besides these few responses, no other creative answers were listed.

In this same survey, 60.9 percent reported that they would like to see their church provide transportation for senior adults.

Finally, in the Sunday School Board survey, the subjects asked what services and activities their church had or should have for shut-ins. They responded to a suggested list in the following way:

church members visit the shut-ins—65.5 percent

provide tape of worship service—49.3 percent

deacons take the Lord's Supper—28.4 percent

telephone reassurance—25 percent

transportation to doctor—20.9 percent

meals on wheels—16.2 percent

handyman service—16.2 percent

adopted grandchildren program—8.1 percent

In these lists, I see a real need for explaining some of these terms to the seniors who try to fill out the questionnaire. For instance, I think a lot of them would be interested in acting as a surrogate grandparent to a child in the church family if they understood the responsibilities it entailed and the joys it would bring. I think they are largely uninformed and, thus, unchallenged.

The Power and Glory of Senior Adults

I know of one situation in which a healthy layman, Jim Little, looked forward to retirement so that he could do more church work. He had been employed by the Internal Revenue Service and had accumulated financial and accounting skills. In addition, he had served as chairman of deacons for a number of years. So he looked forward to acting as a kind of volunteer minister of education.

About the same time that his retirement took place, the pastor he had worked with left; and a younger pastor accepted a call to the church. The newly retired man and the new pastor couldn't understand each other. The older man said that his visits to the church office seemed to be interpreted as interference and meddling. As a consequence, he quit going by the church office and eventually dropped out of worship service attendance until another pastor came on the scene. The tragedy of that situation was that so few senior adults ever volunteer for service of that nature; it was a shame to let that power go unused.

So, senior friends, you are entering a new day of service. When you contrast the lethargy of the past with the needs of the present, you want to volunteer. When you consider the cultural straitjacket of the past in contrast with the biblical meaning of *elder*, you want to act. When you contrast the discrimination against age in the past along with the present opportunity for senior adults to exert their power, you are thrilled with the possibilities. Senior adult, you can have an impact. You can realize some of the divine power and glory; it can be yours. You can grow bold. You can have a unique influence. You can have senior impact. You can enlarge your world.

During my last pastorate, a seven-year sojourn in North Carolina, I dreamed of many projects the church could undertake. At deacons' meetings I tossed out many ideas—some of which they liked but most of which they didn't care for. The one idea that really caught hold, however, didn't come from me, their pastor. It came from a fellow deacon. Mr. M. W. Knott, a man in his sixties, pointed out a way that our church could provide a service and make an impact on the community. He suggested that we study the idea of a day-care center for children of working mothers. The first mention of the idea caused some blinks of incomprehension and some puzzled glances. But for several meetings after that, he brought up the idea and encouraged the deacons to think positively about the project.

Of course, such a project in an urban area might have been quite simple. But carrying out the idea in a small, conservative town seemed quite shocking to some members of the congregation. If the idea had come from an outsider, like the pastor or a new member, it probably would have been rejected. But the idea came from an older member. Mr. Knott had served as a Sunday School teacher of the senior adult men. He had been chairman of the deacons on several occasions. He knew the membership of the church, and they knew him. It was his quiet, influential way of explaining the situation that brought the matter to consideration in church business meeting and ultimate approval.

The process of getting it adopted wasn't easy. Some

old-timers said a fence around the play area would destroy the beauty of the church grounds. Others raised the ugly rumor of little black children mixed in with white ones. But Mr. Knott handled all of these obstacles in his patient, Christian way. He also set an example by making a special gift to the center and offering his own carpentry and electrical skills as they were needed.

Why do I tell you this story of the day-care center? Simply to show that a concerned senior adult was able to get something done. He had the contacts and resources to do something I never could have done. Mr. Knott wasn't content to let his Sunday School teaching be the total expression of his Christian faith. He wanted to know that his church was meeting human needs in the community. He went out on a limb. He made a few people mad. But he was responsible for causing the most important project during my pastorate with that church.

Since then he has died. If I could have been at his funeral, I would have said, "Do you want to see Mr. Knott's memorial? Look around you."

People could have seen a chain link fence—not to mar the aesthetics of the property, but to keep the preschoolers from harm. Beyond that they would have seen happy children playing with each other or talking with kind, Christian teachers. All of this occurred because a senior adult exerted his power. And in my way of thinking, he deserved some glory for it.

2
Jesus Doesn't Want You for a Doormat

Somewhere along the way, we've gotten our directions mixed up. Many of us have ended up out on the veranda of passivity—thinking we were serving our Master. We've lounged in the hammock of pietism when we should have been pushing the wheelbarrow of service.

Most senior adults have feared the label of "activist." They haven't wanted to convey an image of offensive behavior. They've accepted insults. They've let people discriminate against them. They've become passive in old age rather than make demands. Does Jesus want this?

No, the Christ who drove money changers out of the Temple and pointed his finger at the hypocrites doesn't expect you to be a doormat. Jesus wants you for a sunbeam—to shine in dark corners of the world and expose evil. He doesn't want you for a doormat.

Meekness Isn't Weakness

Of course, one way we got mixed up on his instructions was our interpretation of the Sermon on the Mount. Our Master had a whole lot to say about avoiding revenge. He made it clear that he didn't want us to strike back, and he encouraged turning the other cheek—a teaching he exemplified at various points in his own life history. But this lack of personal animosity has cut the ethical nerve for many Christians—especially older ones. They feel they are serving Jesus when they refuse to make any ripples—when they refuse to take a difficult ethical stand.

But go back to the Sermon on the Mount: Recall that Jesus said, "Blessed are the meek" (Matt. 5:5). Look at the word for meekness. We've confused meekness with weakness. Not so with the Master. He used the idea of meekness to mean teachable. Jesus wanted disciples who weren't self-assertive in their egotistical arrogance. He wanted teachable persons of humble trust.

Recall that the Old Testament calls Moses the meekest man in all the earth. (See Num. 12:3.) Certainly that great lawgiver was no spineless Caspar Milquetoast. He blazed with anger on occasion, but he also wept tears of intercession for his people.

Every meek person of the Bible, whether in the New Testament or Old, was a person who wasn't self-centered. If he got angry, it wasn't because of personal pique. He grew angry when God's children were being mistreated. This is the area where a senior adult can become a modern-day Moses.

In every community, human lives still exist in bondage—bound to superstition, to laziness, to ignorance. People are still victims of stereotyping—they're dismissed as unimportant because they're old. Other elderly people are victimized by landlords, merchants, door-to-door salesmen, and young punks. These older Americans—God's children—need attention. They need some God-called leader to release them. Some senior adult can lead a crusade for a modern exodus. Remember, the secret is selfless anger.

When you take Moses as your model, you'll find yourself taking affirmative action for others. Now this kind of behavior has scared you in the past, but it could produce just the opposite effect. You've been afraid you would offend people, but you'll find that you gain respect from them.

An interesting study at the University of Kansas tested the reactions people have to an older person acting assertively. A group of 120 subjects read a story about a woman seventy-six years of age badgering a store manager. Another group of 120 read the same story except that the woman's age was thirty-six. Those who read about the older woman formed more favorable impressions than did the ones who read about the younger woman. This study and similar ones show that when older persons violate the stereotype for their age, the public reacts with favorable responses.

A similar test using a film was carried out at the University of Southern California. Eighty persons viewed a film of a person returning defective merchandise to a store clerk. Half the viewers saw a film in which a young actress played the role, and the others saw an older actress return the merchandise. The older actress was rated just as high as the younger one.

Both these studies suggest that when an older person acts assertively, people show respect. The older person can in this way minimize some of the negative perceptions of the aged.

When you take Moses as your model, you'll find that you'll be making the best use of your time. The great liberator of God's children didn't have time to kill. An older man today who gets involved in helping others won't spend all of his time in front of a TV set. An involved and active older woman won't allot all of her time to playing cards.

The active person will also discover less egocentricity in his or her life. Moses acted on behalf of others. So did Barnabas. So did Jesus. There is no limit to the amount of good that could be done in the world if nobody cared who got the credit.

Six Do's for Christian Action

1. Choose a subject that bugs you. Just look around. Maybe your senior adult Sunday School class has been assigned a room at the top of a flight of steps, but youth have been given one on the lower floor. Maybe there are some potholes in a parking lot where senior adults might fall. All around, you can find wrongs against older people. These could be changed if somebody cared enough to do something about them.

2. Conduct a fact-finding operation. First of all, see if you are wrong. When you know you're not, move ahead at full speed in your investigation. For instance, maybe you want to discover how people get their view of older people. Look at the schoolbooks and see the image they're projecting of older adults. Or clip materials from the newspapers. See what the comics are saying. All of this evidence would be good to present to an editor or a school board.

3. Challenge the stereotypes. For instance, an old idea is that a woman never tells her age. You can show the absurdity of that custom by telling your age and showing that nobody will think less of you—in fact, you'll feel more released. Another stereotype is that a person should retire at age sixty-five. Lots of people are challenging that concept, and you won't be alone if you do.

4. Establish your own power base. Build up a network of goodwill. Have you ever thought of taking a teenager to dinner? Let him choose the place—not a place where he might be embarrassed by being seen by friends—but an out-of-the-way place that would have plenty of good, filling food. That teenager might get you in touch with adolescent friends and give you some real help in getting an unpopular idea across. Of course, your network of power begins in your own circle of friends. When you want somebody to give you some moral help, ask your own best friend. Start with friends, but expand to get others involved.

5. Learn that there's power in numbers. I heard a woman in my church, Claudia Maddox, say about violence on TV: "It's not just me sitting there objecting. It is Foy Valentine and Harry Hollis (outspoken ethical leaders of the denomination) doing everything they can to get Southern Baptists marshaled against the aggressive acts you see in your home on your screen." The people who make laws in Washington have always known that numbers of people could exert power—all the way from defeating a candidate at the polls to writing a few letters of complaint that cause a change of a congressman's vote on an important issue.

6. Never underestimate the power of determination. Who would have thought a few years ago that just because a black woman refused to go to the back of a bus in Alabama, the whole social structure of the country would be changed? A few people were determined to change the structure in a nonviolent way, and they sang "We Shall Overcome" until they did. That same kind of determination was exerted earlier in India and changed society there. That same kind of determination can work for you. But only if you feel strongly enough about a matter to hang in there until your goal is reached.

Six Don't's

1. Don't use offensive terminology. Once when I was serving on the interdenominational Committee on Uniform Series, the Baptist groups got together and discussed an idea. But the person who reported back to the other denominational representatives called the result "the report from the Baptist caucus." That last word had such negative overtones that people voted down the resolution. I couldn't blame them.

2. Don't make nonnegotiable demands. Take a tip from a skilled negotiator. One of Henry Kissinger's techniques was to give in on several minor items to look flexible. He looked for insignificant points of agreement so that he could report a "productive session." If you don't win a whole loaf of bread, you can live on half a loaf for quite a while.

3. Don't work for a selfish motive. If you sell property to the city, you have a profit motive and can't call it

charity. So don't expect praise from others or a warm feeling within yourself if money is involved. The best motivation for elder impact comes from championing the cause of someone else. (My favorite character in the Bible is Barnabas; he was always helping somebody else— speaking up to defend Paul, taking John Mark as his traveling companion, and performing other such good deeds.)

4. Always be courteous. You will show the love of Christ more when you use firm kindness than when you get angry and belligerent. As the old saying goes: You can catch more flies with honey than with vinegar.

5. Go to the top or as near the top as possible. In writing a letter of complaint, you will do well to address a letter to the president of a company. (You'll see more about this idea in chapter 4.)

6. Never undercut the influence of an institution for a short-term goal. When I was a hospital chaplain in Louisville, Kentucky, I saw two different approaches: the news media and the Christian laypersons' group of the Louisville Area Council of Churches. The latter group took the advice of George Stoll never to go to the news media with a criticism of an institution but to take up any grievance in a quiet way with the administrator. While I lived in Louisville, the newspapers took a different approach. Reporters would take an event, such as a patient's death in the emergency room, to provide headlines and suggest negligence. A series of similar events, given an exposé treatment, began to undercut the confidence people had in the hospital. I advise you, as a concerned senior, to work within the institutions for inner reform.

Become a Christian Advocate

OK, if Jesus doesn't want you for a doormat, what does he want you to be? A Christian activist. If you don't like that name, call yourself a senior Samaritan.

Do you know the word *advocate?* It means one who pleads the cause of another. If you were in legal trouble, you'd want a good lawyer to plead your case. When you went to court, you'd want a good advocate.

Senior adults are in trouble—not legal trouble but social trouble. Society has pushed them aside and taken advantage of them too long. It's time now for some advocates for the aging to come forth and plead for their cause.

Thank God, several such people have moved out on the stage of today's thinking. They're defending older people who've been accused without a trial and relegated into stereotypes of feeble senility.

Of all the advocates I can think of, my mind focuses on one—a skinny young man in his twenties, with eyes like chunks of coal in a snowman's face but with a vote-getting smile and a heart that beats for senior adults— Gary Cook. Back when he was a seminary student in Louisville, he began to investigate what America's largest Protestant denomination was doing for the aged. He was appalled at the scarcity of programs and the lack of emphasis on senior adulthood. He didn't keep quiet about it.

In the peculiar democracy that characterizes Southern Baptist life, he stepped to the podium before ten thousand messengers of the Southern Baptist Convention, meeting in Portland, Oregon. Denominational bigwigs

on stage and housewives in printed dresses and ranchers
in double-knit suits in the audience listened. Gary called
for attention to and respect for the aging. He asked for
a study. He had reached out for the rope that had been
hanging there; he rang the bell. The 1973 Convention
voted overwhelmingly for senior adults, resulting in a
1974 Conference on Aging. Dreams materialized!

From that 1974 conference repeated calls for a senior
adult magazine echoed. Such an interest caused the Sunday School Board to schedule such a magazine and to
turn to me because I had been doing some consumer
interviews on what people wanted in a senior adult publication. I became the first editor of *Mature Living*. I am
grateful to Gary for calling for that Conference on Aging
that resulted in the magazine to which I am devoting
my life.

Gary has continued to be an advocate for the aging.
He went to Texas to get further training at the seminary
in Fort Worth. (The Southwestern Baptist Theological
Seminary there offers more courses on aging than any
other theological school in the world.) He also did gradu-
ate work in gerontology at North Texas State University.
He served for two years as a pastor in McGregor, Texas,
leading his congregation in a Meals on Wheels program.
He got the local Rotary Club to take an interest in the
local rest home.

Gary now teaches in the field of gerontology at Baylor
University, Waco, Texas. He serves on several denominational committees with people much older than he. Gary
is trying to marshal all the lay and ministerial forces possible to become advocates for the aging. May his tribe
increase.

3
Set Your Goals

Recently, when I was in the Nashville airport to meet my son, Warren, on his return from the Holy Land, I noticed another young man. He was carrying a silver loving cup about twenty-four inches high. My son recognized him—Darrell Waltrip—and went over to introduce himself.

The previous day that young racing driver had maneuvered his car to victory in the Darlington 400. I'm sure that as he zoomed ahead of the other speeding cars, he must have thought about the beautiful silver prize and the money that went with it. He had a goal before him.

Maybe you would accomplish more in the race of life if you had a goal before you.

The apostle Paul had a goal: "But this one thing I do, forgetting those things which are behind, and reaching forth unto those things which are before, I press toward the mark for the prize of the high calling of God in Christ Jesus" (Phil. 3:13–14). Using the language of the athlete, he was straining every nerve and muscle to push ahead. The murderer-turned-missionary didn't look back—either to admire his past laurels or to concern himself with competitive racers trying to surpass him. His main goal was doing God's will.

Barriers to Goal Setting

At this stage in life, you find many people who want to set your goals for you. Your children or grandchildren try it. Your neighbors, your best friends, your spouse—none of them knows what goes on inside that precious, antique head of yours. God has given you the freedom to make your own decisions, and he doesn't want anybody taking that freedom away. He wants you to direct your own life. So learn to say no to bossy, authoritarian people who try to manipulate your life. Let them know you can make your own decisions. Tell them, "That's why God has given me a brain—to use it."

Another barrier is your own pessimism. Something inside you wants to say, "There's little I can do. I've spent my energy in raising my family and working in the church. Now let somebody else set goals for changing the world; I'm too old and tired to be bothered with it."

Before you denigrate yourself (put yourself down), stop to think about the influence of one person. When you see the potentiality of your life, you can have the aplomb of Archimedes. After developing the principle of the fulcrum he said, "Give me a place to stand, and I can move the world."

You, too, can create a world, enlarge a world, move a world. Think of how gladiatorial games were finally ended. Even after Christian churches were built all over Italy, fun-loving Romans still enjoyed the barbarous combats. But in A.D. 404, as the gladiators were lining up, a monk named Telemachus rushed out into the arena. He commanded the fighters in the name of Christ to desist. The spectators howled. The gladiators turned on the resister, executed him, and proceeded with the combat. But the spectators went away from that place shocked and questioning. The games were soon outlawed—all because of the influence of one man who dared to speak out.

Your single vote can be meaningful. One vote brought California into the United States. One vote elected Oliver Cromwell to the "Long Parliament" and sent Charles I to the scaffold. One vote elected Governor Morton of Massachusetts in 1839, defeating the orator Edward Everett. One vote in a special electoral commission decided who would be president in 1876—Rutherford B. Hayes.

Strength in Numbers

Some goals, however, call for more than an individual. They command the combining of forces into a power bloc. Does that idea turn you off?

Older people feel a need to cooperate, but they are uncertain about joining an activist group. When asked if there is a real need for people to join together to work toward improving the conditions and social status of older Americans, 70 percent of the population over sixty-five said yes. Yet when asked about their interest in joining an organized group to work for these same goals, less than 20 percent would join. About half would support the goals without joining.

Most older church members from rural areas don't appreciate the history of organized labor. Church members know of the inconvenience, higher prices, and occasional violence that general strikes have caused. They've been unsympathetic. What they don't know is that the Medicare and Medicaid programs have resulted from the continuous lobbying and pressure from labor. Before any senior adult groups exerted any influence on the issue, the AFL-CIO advocated a strong federal program to help the nation's elderly. Even with its flaws and inequities, the aid has been a literal lifesaver for many older Americans.

Whether you agree with the labor movement or not, you can learn a lesson of accumulated power from it. When several people combine their strength, the sum is greater than the parts.

For instance, consider the average church choir. A bunch of mediocre voices produces a glorious sound for the glory of God. When senior adults get together and set goals for God's work, a magnificent harmony will result.

A goal, according to the well-known educator Robert Mager, helps you to define success. When you have selected a success goal, you can find ways to achieve it and can know when you have achieved it.

A goal gives a purpose in life. When you achieve a goal you build your self-esteem. This building of good feeling about yourself acts as a reward—a reinforcer—and makes it easier to progress to the next goal.

A part of your goal setting fits right in with the Sermon on the Mount. Jesus advised you to be grown up, mature, and progressing in life's purity. He said, "Be ye therefore perfect, even as your Father which is in heaven is perfect" (Matt. 5:48).

Conjure up an idealized image of yourself. When you hold such a goal before your eyes, you can discover little ways each day that you can move toward it. Of course, with human nature being as it is, you will have many setbacks and reversals. Moral perfection isn't attainable in this life. But to have a goal of a thousand and miss it by a unit is better than having a goal of a hundred and achieving it, according to Robert Browning.

In 1972 Maggie Kuhn convened the Gray Panthers to liberate older people from society's paternalism and oppression that kept them powerless. She claims to be a woman of religious convictions. Even if you disagree with her, you can admit that she has based her goals on Christian principles. "Age makes no difference in serving the Lord and humanity," she has said. She continues to call for creative new ministries by pastors and lay people. "Response to these new ministries could renew and energize congregational life—creating a social force to be compared only with the Protestant Reformation." [1]

A Goal of Conquering Fear

A Texan said to a Californian: "Aren't you afraid to live in California because of earthquakes?"

The Californian said, "You live in a place where they have frequent tornadoes. Are you afraid of them?" When the answer came back no, the person from the West Coast said, "I don't think of earthquakes all the time either. You don't let tornadoes spoil your day, and I don't let earthquakes spoil mine."

Some senior adults are afraid of being a victim of crime. They hear of an incident in their neighborhoods or read of an isolated case in the newpapers. Then they wonder: "Will I be next?" In the Harris survey for the National Council on the Aging, some people over sixty-five reported fear of crime to be a very serious or somewhat serious problem in their lives.

According to Henry F. McQuade, deputy administrator of the Law Enforcement Assistance Administration, older people are less likely to be victimized than young persons. For instance, he showed that in crimes of violence, the elderly rate of eight victimizations per one thousand compares to thirty-two per one thousand for younger people. In crimes of theft, the seniors had twenty-two per one thousand, compared to ninety-one per one thousand for the general population. Household crimes were fifty-five per one thousand for the aged compared to ninety-one per one thousand for the general population. (Only in purse snatching were the figures equal.) So senior adult worries about crime are not exactly realistic, and older people squander a lot of mental energy on this fear.

After you have overcome your own fear, you can help others do the same. A couple of older women in a large city decided that their neighborhood wasn't safe. Did they move out? Indeed not. Each afternoon at sunset they went out for a walk on the streets. Why? They knew if other people saw two elderly women walking, they'd figure it was safe. Then other people did start walking, and it became safer just by weight of numbers.

Anybody Can Set Goals

Goal setting is more than theory and philosophy. The women had a goal of a safe neighborhood. They studied the situation, set a goal, and did something about it.

You can do the same—maybe your problem isn't neighborhood fear. (A survey in Minneapolis, for instance, showed that most senior citizens are scattered around the city and its suburbs rather than being concentrated in a few unsafe neighborhoods.)

In this day of emotional isolation, an older man had a goal of neighborhood unity. He studied the need and acted to achieve his goal. He went around his neighborhood and took color slides of the children. Later he had a showing for the kids and their parents—he brought together a bunch of strangers. They left his home neighbors.

Any person could try this same kind of activity with any sort of photo equipment. It wouldn't have to be expensive. You could try this idea and maybe at the same time introduce a backyard Bible study.

You might want to tackle a problem of an entirely different nature, something that plagues many senior adults, such as fear of being sent to a nursing home. Statistics show that you're wrong to harbor that fear. Only fifteen out of one hundred people will ever have to go to a nursing home. The other eight-five will never go. Chances are you'll be in the group of eighty-five.

But even if you aren't, you can carry resources into any situation that can take you through it. After all, you've weathered the depression and World War II and a whole lot of other turmoil over the years. You've developed ways of coping. So I ask you, Why are you ready to wave the white flag of surrender about a nursing home? You can face that fear by saying to yourself: *I'll probably never need to go. Maybe I'll be one of the eighty-five. But if I do have to go, I'll adjust, make friends of the residents and staff, and be an influence for God and for what is right.*

Ethel Lee, a woman in Winston-Salem, North Carolina, was asked if she would try out an idea of teaching a Sunday School class in a nursing home one Sunday. She did. She liked it. The patients liked it. She went back each week for six years. Then at seventy-nine years of age, she decided to enter a church-sponsored retirement home. At her new residence she inaugurated a regular devotional service and finds great satisfaction in sharing the insights she learned during her years of volunteer service.

Another goal is to help people in need. Many widows are alone and need little chores done for them. The deacons of Grand Avenue Baptist Church, Fort Smith, Arkansas, took seriously what the Bible says about helping widows. They set a goal of looking after the needs of widows and disabled older persons. A study showed that they had one hundred widowed and disabled older persons in their membership.

They suggested a goal of establishing the "Helping Hand Ministry." After the goal was presented to the church, more than one hundred men, women, and youth volunteered to help. These workers help with transportation, emergency plumbing, carpentry, nursing care, and even painting a house occasionally.

A church member who got excited about the idea of helping donated a delivery truck from his grocery business. Other members gave tools and equipment.

Senior Adult Sunday School directors Bill and Wilma Yocum head up the "Helping Hand Ministry." Any calls to the church office are relayed to the Yocums. Every day brings some new kind of request for assistance.

Another group set a goal of helping. The two-thousand-member First Church of the Nazarene, Bethany, Oklahoma, has a senior adult program that goes beyond just having a good time. Catchy names and feelings of responsibility make the activities a success in ministry.

For example, Sunshine Sams (senior adult men) and Sals (senior adult ladies) of the First Church of the Nazarene fulfill social and fellowship needs in nursing care homes and in private residences of shut-ins. They help persons in need and their families, too.

Helping Hannahs and Homers supervise the church pantry. They distribute food, clothing, and furniture. They also assist with medicines and cash gifts to meet emergency needs.

These Nazarenes also have a group called Hallelujah Hatties and Henrys. They are sensitive to the spiritual needs of the shut-ins and the disabled. They help shut-ins to write letters. They read aloud to them, they conduct Bible study for them, and they send birthday and anniversary greetings.

These activities didn't happen spontaneously. They resulted from older people seeing some needs and setting goals for meeting those needs. When senior adults, as individuals or groups, set goals, they are following the example of their Master and Friend.

4
Things You Thought You'd Never Do

Few people give any thought to making preparation for the later years. Suddenly a working person retires. A housewife finds herself widowed. Sunrise and sunset have suddenly brought the senior years. I agree with Paul Tournier, who claims that aging takes a lifetime of preparation.

But in case you haven't thought ahead or prepared for these unique years, it's still not too late. Getting your emotions straight is the biggest task. If you can look on aging as a part of God's plan and find opportunities to work for others, you'll be well on your way to making a success of the harvest years.

I'd like for you to keep an open mind to some of the things I want to suggest in this book, and, in particular, in this chapter.

Intergenerational Activities

A marvelous way to enlarge your world is to associate with other age groups besides your own. Many grandparents and great-grandparents receive more opportunities than they need to baby-sit. They want other contacts. They'd like some meaningful association with teenagers, but these are more difficult to achieve. One of the new interests in secular education and in church work is intergenerational activities.

Some state governments are hiring foster grandparents to work with emotionally disturbed and other types of institutionalized children. The church has an interest in such children and could provide workers without pay. Many older Christians enjoy the opportunity to play games with and to teach children with various degrees of retardation. They'd also enjoy the chance to be a foster grandparent to a normal kid whose real grandparents live too far away to see very often.

Another approach is the church-related social event. Many churches plan an annual Valentine banquet in which the youth host the event, present the program, and honor the senior adults as the guests. This kind of dinner can be planned any time during the year, and both age groups will enjoy it. A senior adult club could do the reverse of this and play host to the teenagers.

Some churches with both senior adult and youth choirs take both of the groups on trips together. The generations mix and learn to appreciate each other better.

A contact between teenagers and senior citizens took place recently in North Carolina, similar to the life review technique mentioned elsewhere in this book. Teenagers interviewed older persons and wrote biographies that emphasized life satisfactions. A total of 360 volunteers from 4-H Clubs, with ages from thirteen to eighteen, took part in the nine-county project.

In one session, a panel of five retirees met with students and answered questions about retirement. In another, students wearing distorted eyeglasses were required to read articles to other students wearing cotton earplugs. Both groups came to appreciate and understand sensory losses in senior adulthood.

Both groups in the North Carolina project came to appreciate the other. The same results were secured in Staten Island, New York, where older people had built up prejudices and fears about the young people they saw on the streets. After the interviews, the older people had a great confidence in the worth of modern, urban teenagers.

Christian youth who have a Christian motivation enjoy working with older persons. Many such teenagers are simply looking for some need they can meet; conversely, many older adults have not because they ask not. If older people would let youth know of their interest in communication, more involvement would take place.

A group of seventeen students from Mississippi College learned about some senior adults—not in their own state or even a neighboring state but in Florida. These young adults went to St. Petersburg, Florida, to work with the older people.

What did they do after they made that long trip, you ask? All sorts of things, really, depending on the individual interests and talents of the youth as they interacted with the older people in the Sunshine State. They entertained with music, drama, and puppets. They had a guitar ministry. They did maintenance work on senior adult housing. They talked with older persons and made them feel important. They carried out the ministry of Christ with attention to the physical needs of the least of his precious children.

Senior adults in Lansing, Michigan, can't say enough good things about the teenagers of their city. Back in 1974, junior high school students wanted to know and to help the residents who were moving into a new apartment complex for senior citizens near their school. Under the direction of a teacher, Jack Cooper, they decided on a food project. They provided fresh produce at wholesale prices. Since then the project has grown to include canned goods, bakery items, eggs, and staples. The older people find it convenient to buy food in small quantities. They like the low prices. They're glad they don't have to worry about transportation.

If your community or church hasn't begun some kind of contact, you might initiate a program. The easiest to start might be a discussion group. My church in Nashville, Immanuel Baptist Church, began such a group several years ago on Sunday nights and called it "Second Family." People such as Albert McClellan, a denominational executive, and Jud Hendrix, now a third grader, enjoyed working on projects together and reporting to the group.

A typical program was on rocks. Each person brought a rock. One child brought a rock from his own backyard; one adult brought one from his travels in the Holy Land. They told about them, passed them around, and felt of them. A brief discussion centered on rocks in the Bible. Refreshments included old-fashioned rock candy.

Are these the only approaches? Besides the intergenerational study group, the choir tours, the foster grandparent program, and the life review/interview, what else can the senior adult do to bring together different age groups? Consider helping with scenery or costumes in a play. Join a club or class with a special interest, such as a photography class or a Sierra Club (to protect wildlife and the environment). Tutor a child who's having trouble with math or a foreign student with English.

These are only a few suggestions. Your imagination can lead you to many other contacts that will enlarge your world. Maybe you'll think of a new approach some morning when you're lying awake at three o'clock or later on a Sunday morning when you're trying not to sleep during a long sermon.

Give and Take Constructive Criticism

Some of the biggest learning experiences in my life have come from people giving me constructive criticism. One of the first funerals I ever conducted was at the Baptist Home for the Aging in Yonkers, New York. After the service was over a fellow church member, Miss Hazard, suggested that I was much too solemn for the occasion. She said, "These people all live within the shadow of death. It doesn't come by surprise. It sometimes comes as a relief and blessing. They need a note of victory sounded in a funeral."

I agreed with her at the moment, and I further recalled her words on subsequent occasions when I conducted a devoted Christian's funeral as a celebration.

But I often learn from criticism. My teachers have offered advice, pointing out faults and stressing my strengths. In this way I learned preaching from my homiletics professor. I am learning the cello from a teacher who points out both strengths and weaknesses. I am grateful for a writing class in which class members read their own compositions and the rest of the class tore them apart. I accepted criticism, and I tried to improve my writing skills. I learn from the critical letters I receive about the magazine *Mature Living*.

You can offer criticism in a helpful way. When you go as a friend, admitting your own faults and wanting to help a person to do better in the future, you'll probably succeed. Now, remember, of course, that when you are free with your words of criticism, you'll probably have some thrown in your direction. Sometimes these come back as a form of retaliation, but you can learn from them—whatever the motivation. At other times when you are generous with your criticism, the other person feels free to tell you something that he or she has hesitated to say but has thought about for a long time. What an opportunity! The channels of communication in friendship can be opened in this manner to both positive and negative feelings. So accept criticism, and learn from it.

If you receive the kind of criticism that is purely negative—a put-down—you don't need to take it. If someone calls you a name or belittles something you try to do, respond with firm but appropriate words. You might say to yourself the familiar words, *God created me, and he didn't make no trash.*

God has given you the right to be yourself, and he doesn't want other people mistreating you. You need to recognize your right and defend it. If you don't defend your right to be yourself, other people will define your role for you and get you to stop being yourself.

Do you have the right to answer honestly when someone asks your opinion? Of course. Do you have the right to disregard what your children tell you to do? Yes. Do you have the right to refuse to go to the same old places that your best friend always wants to go? Yes. Do you have the right to tell a doctor or a nurse not to call you by your first name? Indeed you do. Do you have the right to ask a doctor or an automobile mechanic to explain his bill? Sure. Do you have the right to ask a person you live with to turn off the TV or to put out a cigarette? Yes, if you give that person the right to say no.

The Art of Complaining

In a list of advice for older persons, a popular magazine put as number 1: Demand, don't whine. This suggestion is similar to my idea of complaining. You complain when you have a big idea. When I was a pastor I got tired of people complaining about the temperature of the air conditioner. I wished they'd complain about something really significant—like the need for recreational equipment for the youth or entrance ramps for wheelchairs.

When you have a complaint, make sure it concerns something important—such as a loose handrail in a building or a person who is being mistreated. You don't need to turn your big guns on little targets.

The best complaints are those that aren't selfish. When a person isn't paid enough and you bring this to public attention, you are helping someone else. When you look over plans for a new building and see that someone has omitted ramps for wheelchairs, you need to complain until that fault is remedied. Sometimes it will take more than one attempt. But remember the old saying: The wheel that squeaks the loudest gets the grease.

Many times your complaint needs to be a letter to a

business. To be effective, the letter must be above the character of a "bedbug letter." In olden times, many hotels and inns received letters of complaints about bedbugs. The letters were so frequent that they received a stock answer. To keep from getting a stock answer today, you should write to the president of the company by name. You can get this information from your public library; look for the big volume called *Standard and Poor's Register of Corporations, Directors and Executives.* It's not a bad idea to send a carbon copy to the vice-president. You'll find those names in the book.

Many people who were born in the early part of this century were reared on the don't-raise-a-fuss philosophy. They were told to wonder, *What will people think of me?* Such people are afraid of looking cheap or cranky; thus, they hesitate to complain. But a person who is a child of God has an obligation to uphold what is right and not to let a willfully dishonest person perpetrate a fraud.

A woman who is an advocate for older people in Louisiana has become known as a complainer (in the best sense of the word). She is assertive (also in the best sense of that word). So she felt it was a compliment when a politician said to her: "You're the flea that makes the dog scratch."

She encourages older people to keep in touch with the state legislature. "If you don't write to the people at the capitol, they'll forget why they're there."

5
You and Politics

Ruth Jenkins hasn't missed voting in an election since she registered back in the 1920s. As a Christian and as a citizen, she takes her voting seriously. But if you ask Ruth about politics she will say, "I don't want to get involved in it." She wants honest officials and good government, but she doubts that she will get either. Furthermore, she's not willing to work for those goals. How do you explain that inconsistency?

She has heard over the years that all politicians are dishonest scoundrels. She hasn't exactly believed it, but she also hasn't refuted the claim. If you asked Ruth to run for an office, she would tell you, "I don't know anything about government. Besides, I'm a woman."

Ruth is unlike the young woman in Tennessee government who wears a T-shirt that reads: "A woman's place is in the house . . . and in the senate."

Many women and older Americans haven't participated in government as much as they could have. Perhaps with more of the insights from both women and older citizens, the political climate of the United States could change.

You a Lobbyist?

American political scientists agree that the lobbyist is an important element of the American democratic process. The lobbyist is one who tries to influence the actions of the legislative and executive branches of the government. Of course, some of these people use unethical methods. But many organizations and individuals try—legally and ethically—to keep the decision makers in Congress aware of what the voter wants.

Another effective way you can operate is through the simple procedure of writing a letter. You don't have to go to Washington to influence public policy. As a voting citizen, you have the right to let your representatives know how you feel on certain issues.

Here are some suggestions about writing your senator or congressman:

1. Write a short, clear letter. Deal with only one issue, not several. Make sure that you know what you are writing about. Don't respond to some rumor you have heard. Be informed on your subject if you expect to make an impression on the decision makers in Washington.

2. Type your letter or have it typed. It will save the people in Washington a lot of time and trouble if they don't have to decipher your handwriting.

3. Be as positive as possible. Praise something the politician has said or done. Express appreciation for a courageous stand or for some help the representative has given.

4. If you want to oppose a position, do so in a logical manner, using polite language and Christian principles.

You will have a better effect if you refrain from name calling and even from threatening to withdraw your vote. Every politician knows your power at the polls without your holding that club over his or her head.

5. Be selective in the issues you speak out on. Try to be consistent. Don't feel that you have to write on every issue, or you will dilute your influence.

6. Write at the best possible time. Don't wait until a bill is brought up to the floor for a vote. Do your work earlier, when it will count for more. Write your elected representative when the bill is pending in committee. To the person who doesn't know Washington, this advice probably sounds stupid. But the person who has visited the Capitol or has talked with the politicians knows that the place to kill a measure or get it amended favorably is in the committee. Your letter will have the most influence at that point.

If you want to write a committee or a member of Congress, use the following addresses:

The Honorable _____ _____
United States Senate
Washington, D.C. 20510

Senate Committee on _____
United States Senate
Washington, D.C. 20510

The Honorable _____ _____
House of Representatives
Washington, D.C. 20515

gress and eleven interns. In recent years over fifty members of Congress sponsor around a hundred interns each May.

When interns aren't in briefing sessions, they sit in on committee hearings and work in the sponsoring member's office. They assist with office duties. They meet with their sponsor and that person's assistant to discuss legislation affecting the elderly. They give their recommendations. They reflect on how older constituents at home feel about specific issues.

Bud Hillis wrote me a letter explaining this marvelous plan, and he pointed out the following: "The end of the two-week internship in Washington is just the beginning of the program. When interns return to their hometowns, they begin to share their experiences and knowledge gained during their stay in Washington."

Mr. Hillis made a similar report on the floor of the House. The *Congressional Record* for June 30, 1977, reports his words to his fellow lawmakers: "But it is not a one-way street; it is equally enlightening to those Members who have taken part. I think they would tell you how we have also learned and how we as Members of Congress have benefited in gaining insights into their particular problems, concerns, and needs as we never have before."

One of the interns from Indiana, Paul Perdiue, from Anderson, said, "Next to my appointment as general manager of the Central Indiana Railway, this was the greatest thing that happened in our life."

Another Indiana couple, Chester and Verle Edwards, said, "We learned through various hearings and briefings about legislative procedures, Older American Act, National Health Insurance, Medicare, Urban Mass Transit, Social Security, SSI and Social Services, and the ACTION programs. We brought back much information and many pictures. Our slide picture story about senior citizen interns has been presented many times to various senior citizen groups."

Two other interns made an interesting observation. This word comes from Dave and Doreen Durlacher of Kansas City, Missouri: "Any American who reaches the age of fifty-five or older has done so by the grace of God, good management, and above average driving skills. For the past fifty years, anyone five years older than we was an older American. The problems in our society that seem to have the greatest impact on the aged are: (1) inflation, (2) medical costs, (3) transportation, (4) crime, (5) housing, (6) nutrition, and (7) our mobile society."

Obviously, the interns and the members of Congress were impressed. This level of contact and interaction needs to be broadened. Is your state represented in the following list of the members of Congress who sponsored interns recently?

House of Representatives

Daniel K. Akaka, HI
Anthony C. Beilenson, CA
Michael T. Blouin, IA
Goodloe E. Byron, MD
Yvonne B. Burke, CA
John L. Burton, CA
E. Thomas Coleman, MO
Robert J. Cornell, WI
Lawrence Coughlin, PA
John H. Dent, PA

Edward J. Derwinski, IL
Robert F. Drinan, MA
Mickey Edwards, OK
Joshua Eilberg, PA
Allen E. Ertel, PA
Billy Lee Evans, GA
David W. Evans, IN
Walter E. Fauntroy, DC
Millicent Fenwick, NJ
Hamilton Fish, Jr., NY

Floyd J. Fithian, IN
Elwood H. Hillis, IN
Harold C. Hollenbeck, NJ
Jack F. Kemp, NY
William M. Ketchum, CA
Martha Keys, KS
Dale E. Kildee, MI
Thomas N. Kindness, OH
Peter H. Kostmayer, PA
Robert Krueger, TX
James Leach, IA
William Lehman, FL
Elliott H. Levitas, GA
Stanley N. Lundine, NY
Andrew Maguire, NJ
James R. Mann, SC
Marc L. Marks, PA
Romano L. Mazzoli, KY
Helen S. Meyner, NJ
Barbara A. Mikulski, MD
Gary A. Myers, PA
John T. Myers, IN
Richard Nolan, MN
James L. Oberstar, MN
George M. O'Brien, IL
Thomas P. O'Neill, Jr., MA
Richard Ottinger, NY
Leon E. Panetta, CA
Edward J. Patten, NJ
Larry Pressler, SD
Joel Pritchard, WA
Albert H. Quie, MN
Charles B. Rangel, NY
Ralph S. Regula, OH
John J. Rhodes, AZ
Frederick W. Richmond, NY
Matthew J. Rinaldo, NJ
J. Kenneth Robinson, VA
Elton Rudd, AZ
Philip E. Ruppe, MI

Richard T. Schulze, PA
Patricia Schroeder, CO
Philip R. Sharp, IN
Paul Simon, IL
B. F. Sisk, CA
Gladys N. Spellman, MD
Newton I. Steers, Jr., MD
Gene Taylor, MO
Jim Guy Tucker, AR
Morris K. Udall, AZ
Bruce F Vento, MN
Wesley Watkins, OK
Theodore S. Weiss, NY
Larry Winn, Jr., KS
Timothy E. Wirth, CO
John W. Wydler, NY
C. W. "Bill" Young, FL

Senate

Wendell Anderson, MN
Lloyd Bentsen, TX
Edward W. Brooke, MA
Clifford P. Case, NJ
Lawton Chiles, FL
Dennis DeConcini, AZ
Robert Dole, KS
Jack Garn, UT
Floyd Haskell, CO
Mark O. Hatfield, OR
Ernest F. Hollings, SC
James A. McClure, IA
Charles Mathias, Jr., MD
Spark M. Matsunaga, HI
Bob Packwood, OR
William V. Roth, Jr., DE
Richard Stone, FL
Strom Thurmond, SC
John Tower, TX
Harrison Williams, Jr., NJ

An increasing number of senior adults want to be involved in the political scene. They realize that to have a part in self-determination, they must become politically activated. Yet they know they can't win alone. They are increasingly turning for help to the people from fifty to sixty-five because these people are already beginning to think about their concerns after they turn sixty-five.

Beyond letter writing and visiting Washington, a deeper level of involvement comes when senior adults decide to jump into the political lake. Some people reach retirement age and realize that for the first time in their lives they have time to run for some office—maybe a local school board or some state offices. They have a little money they don't mind investing in a cause, and they have reached the age in which they don't care if someone gets offended by a statement or an action.

Isabella Cannon was one of those persons. She was seventy-three when she ran for mayor of the city of Raleigh, North Carolina, in 1977. Some people thought she didn't have a ghost of a chance. But with hard work and a corps of dedicated volunteer workers, she was elected mayor. The five-foot, ninety-five-pound politician said, "I owe my success to a coalition that cut across age, race, and economic lines."

Says Mayor Cannon: "Older people have two priceless assets—time and a wealth of experience. Public service is a good field for sharing those gifts."

Getting a Whole State Involved

The more people involved in goal setting, the bigger the goal can become. Take Wisconsin, for instance. Back in 1974, a handful of people were interested in some senior centers for the state and suggested that a sum of $500,000 be appropriated. The suggestion was taken seriously by a few lawmakers in the capitol at Madison, but little happened.

Then James Sykes and John Shier began to work with a coalition of aging groups. They expanded the group to include virtually every active aging organization, club, and agency in the state. From this coalition came a statewide senior citizen consensus. The five issues that demanded attention were these: senior centers, nutrition, transportation, home health care, and increased tax relief.

A letter-writing campaign to Gov. Patrick Lucey produced thousands of requests for the governor to include these five areas in his budget proposals. Then senior citizens appeared in town hall meetings held throughout the state and spoke for these same matters.

In seeking their goal, the coalition stressed the large number of senior adults who were registered voters. Another theme was that aging programs are in the public interest. They claimed that the needs of the elderly are the needs of the public as it ages. They tried to point out that senior citizens were not a special interest group seeking selfish goals. The coalition of older groups emphasized that when the government does something for the senior citizens, it does something that will help everybody sooner or later.

Next, the goal seekers across the state planned a "Senior Citizens' Day at the State Capitol." The event was publicized and glamorized. Excitement built. By the time the rally was scheduled to begin, a steady stream of buses had encircled the capitol. Five thousand senior adults from across the state of Wisconsin filled the rotunda. Governor Lucey said it was the largest crowd he'd ever seen at the capitol. He stated that he wanted each of the state's seventy-two counties to have a senior center. Then he promised to fight for his recommendation. The crowd roared with approval.

Then the elders themselves spoke. They presented thoughtful, well-prepared testimonies. Their eloquence surprised one another. Their anecdotes and remembrances made the occasion one to remember.

The legislature responded by passing the proposals. Rather than the $500,000 originally requested, the lawmakers allocated the following: $2 million for senior centers; $2.6 million for specialized transportation services; a state supplement to expand the federal nutrition program by 60 percent; state grants to create and expand home health agencies; a $63 million increase in total property tax relief benefits that could reduce senior citizen tax liabilities by up to 60 percent.

The long campaign brought a victory. But it demonstrated to the senior citizens of Wisconsin, as well as every other state, that future goals can be realized when lawmakers are educated to the needs and convinced of the pressure that older voters can exert. The people of Wisconsin did nothing unethical; on the contrary, they made democracy work. They encouraged elected officials to be sensitive to the needs of the people.

When senior adults want to influence a politician's decisions, they can appeal to that person's public image. Twenty older citizens who felt strongly about an issue corralled Governor Reagan between the glass doors of San Francisco's Ferry Building. They cut him off from his bodyguards and advisers. Television news cameras recorded his embarrassment for millions of California viewers just before the 1970 election.

What caused these kind old people to act in such a rash way? For two years Governor Reagan had vetoed a measure that would pass Social Security payment increases on to 315,000 aged poor persons. Under state law, the increase was regarded as extra income and thus deducted from state Old Age Social Security checks. At this confrontation, the governor was faced with picket signs, whirring cameras, and shouts of "Going to sign the bill this time?"

The pressure worked, and within a few days he had signed the legislation. The poor people received a $7.50 per month increase. Note that the people who exerted this power didn't do so for a selfish reason. They were advocates for ones who needed more resources for living. Advocacy involves bringing helpful information to lawmakers, policymakers, the general public, and senior citizens. It also involves applying pressure. Shrewd advocates will not waste time on trivial issues. They will aim at strategic issues and marshal their forces for a victory.

6
You and the Media

If you want to enlarge your world, start with the news and entertainment media. Does that sound as farfetched as a rocket trip to the moon? Pessimistic Polly said, "The only time you'll ever read my name in the paper is when I die and get in the obituary column."

Optimistic Otho said, "I have a great idea, and I hope to see it on radio, TV, in newspapers, national magazines, on records, tapes, billboards, and everywhere." Perhaps each went to an extreme. They needed to face the idea of communications realistically.

Write a Letter

I frequently tell aspiring authors that the easiest way to get published is to write a letter to your newspaper editor. You won't get paid in money, but a lot of people will see your letter and think your thoughts. What better pay could you ask?

I'd like to challenge you to write a letter or a series of letters. The reader's response column could be the platform for getting your idea across.

If you want to take an affirmative stand, write to a newspaper. Make your letter brief and to the point. Make some different kind of statement that will elicit attention. Keeping it from being drab. Spice it up with some word pictures. Of course, this pictorial approach is one of the Gray Panther's strong points. Their leader, Maggie Kuhn, instead of saying the world treats us with paternalism, says the world treats us like wrinkled babies. Instead of saying America is wasteful, she says we have the Detroit syndrome. You can develop such word pictures that excite people. Then you can influence public opinion through the letters-to-the-editor column.

I wrote to *Time* magazine once. Not only did they publish my letter but they sent a telegram to notify me.

Besides that part of the newspapers, you could contribute to other pages. Many a harried editor is just waiting for a story on older people who are different. He has plenty of stories on golden wedding anniversaries, but he has few on seniors doing the unusual. The editor would love a story on a woman who entered politics after she retired and was elected to the school board. Newspaper readers would like to hear of older groups who are helping little children with reading problems or of senior adults who are going back to the college campuses as students.

Editors pay no attention to a dog-bites-man story but still get excited over a man-bites-dog story. In other words, the item has to be unusual to get reader attention and to make an impact. Keep your senses ready for a good story. So if one of your jogging acquaintances participates in the senior adult olympics, let the paper have the story. Or if a woman you know makes a quilt by charging church members to sign it, then turns around and gives both the quilt and the money to the church—there's a story. Both this man and this woman did something unusual. They bit a dog, so to speak; and the busy world looked up to see what happened.

I'd like to encourage you to write. You can break into print if you have an ounce of talent and several pounds of persistence.

During my eight years as an editor, I've looked over lots of material. Some of it made me laugh. Some of it made me sigh. But most of it put me to sleep. I saw some common mistakes. They also cropped up when I've talked with aspiring writers at conferences I've conducted.

Out of this background, I've formed some ideas that should help you enlarge your world by writing for religious publications. You will make a sale and also convince your readers when you avoid the following common errors.

Seven Deadly Sins of Religious Writing

1. Not exciting. I consider this the worst sin. How could anyone make the thrilling story of the Bible sound dull? It takes a dried-up spirit to do that. You know what I mean. You've read religious articles, seen religious films, and heard religious talks that put you to sleep. They were boring.

When you write, you don't have to make your material boring. People who'll read your writing will be ones who watch TV (your chief competitor). And if you don't grab your readers within the first paragraph or two, they will drop your words and turn on the TV set.

One reason I felt a strong impulse to become an editor of Sunday School lessons when I was invited to back in 1970 was that I had read many lessons that had struck me as dull and monotonous. I wanted a chance to train writers and produce lessons that would thrill and inspire. I enjoyed six years of trying to produce sparkling, uplifting Bible study materials. Then I turned to a magazine that has entertained and inspired a growing number of senior adults. (Young adults have also discovered it and have started to subscribe.)

2. No target. If you aim at nothing, you'll usually hit it. Some writers aim at everybody, as if they addressed an article to "All you folks out there in magazineland."

I don't advise writing with a group in mind, not even to a couple. I write to one person. Why? Only one person at a time will read my words, and I want that one reader to feel that I am carrying on a personal conversation with him or her.

Before you can write to one person, you need to know the target audience that the person is part of. If you are writing for *Mature Living* or the Methodist's *Mature Years,* you can know that 60 percent of the audience have only a high school education or less. These older people didn't have the opportunities for study that young people have today. The writer, therefore, will write in a simple, conversational style. The writer who wants to make contact with and give inspiration to an older person will avoid complex sentence structure and an exotic vocabulary. The skillful writer will write to express, not impress.

3. Not researched. Few devotional articles, Sunday

School lessons, or religious book manuscripts ever arrive at the publishing houses with Scripture passages quoted correctly. Lazy writers quote from memory and usually make mistakes. The careful writer will look up a passage from the Bible and quote accurately.

The same approach holds for spelling. You should look up a word in the dictionary. Even if you are reasonably sure of its spelling, you could be wrong. So check and double-check.

Many writers would produce better material if they spent some time in a public or church library beforehand. Basic research is at the foundation of every good piece of writing.

Before you call me crazy, let me remind you that all research isn't done with books. Some of it is done with people. You have read articles that never quoted from a book but quoted ordinary people on the street. That, too, is a kind of research. One author wrote a piece for *Mature Living* on his interviews with six retired executives and what they are doing with their skills and energies now. He talked with only six people, but that was research.

4. Not edited. You sin against the editor when you pull a sheet out of the typewriter and zip it along to him or her. Just as a bulb needs a germination period before it produces a beautiful janquil or tulip, so you need to let your thoughts germinate. Go back a second time when the material is cold and look at it through the cold, impartial eyes of a stranger. Edit. Make changes. Write a second, third, or maybe even an eighth draft before you send it off. You'll improve your chance of getting pub-

lished if you do your own editing and quit expecting the busy editor to do it for you.

5. Not conversational. I once told a group of aspiring authors, "Write like you talk." A prissy little woman who had taught English told me it should be "as you talk." "No," I replied. "That's not the way I talk. I think you need to write like you talk."

People have come to expect an encyclopedia, a biblical commentary, or a scholarly paper to be written in stilted English. Right, and that's just the reason these pieces aren't more widely read. A magazine like the *Reader's Digest* uses an informal approach and attracts millions of readers.

6. Not true-to-life. When people write something for a religious publication, they shift gears in their thinking—they go into reverse. They write about cannibals in darkest Africa or bonnie wee lassies or something else from the Victorian era.

Modern readers want to know how to face life now. They have problems with arthritis, with grandchildren, with self-esteem, and with other problems. They're looking for answers. They like how-to-articles and interviews with celebrities. They want a writer to use the language of today, even in a piece about eternal values.

7. No take-away. Just as people don't like a sermon without an application, they don't want an article without some practical conclusion. As the managing editor of *Guideposts* said to me one time, "Every article in *Guideposts* must have take-away." People have come to expect some insight that will improve their lives from every article in that magazine.

My friend, if you avoid these seven deadly sins of religious writing, you will have a good chance of selling your thoughts to a religious publishing house.

Here are some addresses you might find helpful:

Religious Magazines for Senior Adults

Mature Living, Sunday School Board of the Southern Baptist Convention, 127 Nineth Avenue, North, Nashville, Tennessee 37234

Mature Years, The United Methodist Publishing House, 201 Eighth Avenue, South, Nashville, Tennessee 37202

Other Magazines for Senior Adults

Best Years, National Association of Mature People, 50 Penn Place, Box 26792, Oklahoma City, Oklahoma 73125

Modern Maturity, American Association of Retired Persons, 215 Long Beach Boulevard, Long Beach, California 90801

Retirement Living, Whitney Communications Corporation, 150 East 58th Street, New York, New York 10022

September Days, Days Inns of America, Inc., 2751 Buford Highway, N. E., Atlanta, Georgia 30324

Your Influence on TV and Radio

Surveys confirm the fact that many senior adults watch TV. Further, they spend a considerable amount of time in front of the tube. Because they comprise a large part of the audience, their feelings should be considered.

Research shows that the public isn't critical of the way

television portrays older people. Perhaps TV maintains the stereotypes the public believes in. Only 12 percent of the steady TV viewers think that programming makes older people look worse than they really are. Most older people are complacent about the way TV portrays them.

Some senior adults have never given any thought to the way age is handled on the screen. Others might have noticed but didn't feel strongly about it; so they raised no fuss.

Many people enjoy watching the antics of Carol Burnett on television. I sometimes enjoy viewing her program—that is, until she and Tim Conway start doing their old-person routines. Audiences howl when the comedians shuffle across the stage and collapse in rocking chairs. I'd like to say to them what Molly used to say on the radio, "'Tain't funny, Magee."

When comedians start to do those old-person characterizations, they cease being funny and start being cruel. Instead of laughing *with* old people, they tend to be laughing at them. I have too many friends who have equilibrium trouble or arthritic pains for me to laugh at TV clowns tottering and shuffling across the stage.

Older Americans can take a stand against any comics who demean and put down older people. They can engage in a media watch—the kind that the Gray Panthers conduct, monitoring to see if older persons are presented in a good light. Then they can send letters of complaint or appreciation to a local TV station (possibly sending carbon copies to the network, to the sponsor, and to the Federal Communications Commission).

Here are some addresses you might find helpful:

• ABC, 1330 Avenue of the Americas, New York, NY 10019

CBS, 51 West 52nd Street, New York, NY 10019

NBC, 50 Rockefeller Plaza, New York, NY 10020

PBS, 485 L'Enfant Plaza S.W., Washington, D.C. 20024

Federal Communications Commission, Washington, D.C. 20554

Two researchers in Utah conducted a study of television programming. They and their helpers sampled programs every day of the week over a six-week period. They discovered something about characters on the tube. The older a man was, the more respect he received. Not so for the female. While men failed only because they were evil, women failed because they were aged.

The study also showed that no characters above sixty were shown to have any romantic interests—thus perpetuating "the myth of the sexless, boring oldster whose inner life is unworthy of interest." [1]

A study of eighty commercials showed that youth was celebrated and older people were depicted as unhealthy, unstylish, and uninteresting.

With all of this negative propaganda, Americans continue to get reinforcement for their negative stereotypes of the aged.

Do you want to do something about the TV picture? Try the positive approach. When you see a program that depicts an older person in a favorable light, write a letter of praise. The station manager will be shocked but pleased and will likely report your response to the network. Also let the sponsor know you approve and will encourage your friends to use the product advertised.

If you see something on TV that offends you, take some action. If the TV show is so repulsive that it knocks you out of your chair, get up and hit back where it hurts— in the area of advertising revenue. As a last resort, threaten sponsors with a boycott of their products if they don't change their program approach. This is one way to get action. A word of caution: you'd better not write in about a program you have just heard about and haven't seen for yourself. You can make yourself look foolish if you don't have all the facts.

These same approaches go for radio. Many people listen to radio when they wake up or just before bedtime or when driving in a car. You can make an impact on radio the same way you do with the TV medium. Write a positive letter of praise and, when necessary, a condemning letter to a sponsor.

Does all this sound too idealistic? Are you afraid you'd never get to first base in the media game? Take heart. Remember that winners never quit, and quitters never win.

Under Federal Communications Commission rules, citizens must be granted air time to discuss local problems. You have three opportunities: you may request air time to discuss a timely local subject, to make announcements about events, or to reply to station editorials or parts of regular news programs that are not objective in dealing with the facts.

Of course, you must submit your presentation in writing. Send an accompanying letter to the station program director and explain what you feel will benefit the listeners or viewers.

The person who communicates finds a feeling of satisfaction. One of the free-lance writers who submits material to *Mature Living* wrote the following to me: "I am enclosing the recent picture you asked for. George took this last month. I hope no more 'laugh lines' have come since then. Could be, though, since I have found a good deal to laugh about" (June Masters Bacher).

Senior adults who use the media to project their thoughts seem to be happy people. Whether you write an article or a letter about a radio/TV program or a letter to an editor, you can enlarge your world and enrich your life.

7
Health, Recreation, and Travel

Take a look at yourself in the mirror. Yep, that's really you. Have you taken care of your body? Have you given yourself some opportunities to travel around and enjoy your world? You can enlarge your world by taking care of your body and by taking it to some new, exciting places.

A ballerina in a recent movie said that since childhood dancing classes her body had tried to rebel against what she wanted it to do. She wouldn't let it. Now that she was on the verge of retirement from the stage, she admitted that her body would no longer follow directions from her mind. Yet she kept on sending it instructions.

Maybe you can sympathize. I can. I started taking cello lessons at fifty-one years of age. I knew what I wanted my fingers to do, but they didn't always play what I told them to. Still I kept practicing, and I'm continuing, just hoping for a breakthrough. I don't make excuses. I just keep sawing away.

The Importance of Exercise

Do you make excuses? You can greatly enlarge your world if you refuse to use age as an excuse for taking no exercise. "I'm too old to jog," one person said to me.

Another said, "If I got on a bicycle, I'd break my neck."
Both statements are exaggerations. But the tragedy of
the health-exercise scene is that many older people aren't
taking the exercises they could. Also, they're not eating
properly.

Two friends who are recreation specialists, Don Mat-
tingly and Bob Sessoms, took a survey of one thousand
persons who attended senior adult Chautauquas at Ridgecrest and Glorieta Conference Centers recently. They
asked what the respondents did for physical exercise.
Here are their surprising answers:

    walking—21 percent
    housework—17.5 percent
    yard work—17 percent
    gardening—9 percent
    calisthenics—8.7 percent
    bicycling—3.4 percent
    golf—2 percent
    swimming—1.5 percent
    bowling—1.5 percent

Other answers included playing with grandchildren,
shopping, fishing, judo, skipping rope, and ironing.

The most surprising (and disappointing) answer on the
survey occurred when 12.7 percent reported that they
took *no* exercise.

Look back over the answers, and you see they're not
too exemplary. Household work has movement, and yard
work is even a bit more strenuous. But these two activities
reported by two of the largest groups do not help the
body gain flexibility, increase circulation, or strengthen
the heart and lungs.

Disciplined walking would be the first activity a person could start in a new program of exercise. Of the people who reported that they walked for exercise, several said they walk from five to nine miles a week. A few even reported up to fifty miles per week. Ask any one of these persons and you will get a testimony of better feeling, better appetite, and less insomnia than nonexercisers.

When the authorities advise walking, they mean brisk walking—not just ambling like a cow in a meadow, but more like a traveler hurrying across an airline terminal lobby to keep from missing a flight. The walker should exercise at least every other day. Then he will find that his heart and lungs get the stimulation they need.

Excuses about walking center around the weather and the danger involved. Well, I know of people who walk the hallways of their church or walk in covered shopping centers on rainy days. I know of older people who walk in pairs, in order to have companionship and safety.

If you want to get more exercise, why don't you talk to your doctor, a high school gym teacher, or a director at a Y or health spa? Get some expert advice about the best kind of exercise program for yourself.

Crafts and Hobbies

I love craft shows. I am glad these exhibits of creativity are becoming more popular all over the country. I enjoy the blown glass and leather goods. I get excited over the old crafts. I like to see someone working on a potter's wheel. I find it fascinating to watch someone at a loom or carving wood or spinning wool or flax.

On the contrary, I hate to hear anybody put down

crafts and hobbies. The detractors call it a kind of "make work." Just something to kill time. I disagree. I think any kind of craft calls for creativity.

Older persons are tempted to say that youth has a monopoly on creativity. The wrinkled man and the gray-haired woman are tempted to abdicate their thrones of creativity.

It's time for senior adults to do some trust-busting on youth's monopoly. Older people have allowed the situation to develop. Call it laziness or whatever you like, but don't call it God's will. The Almighty gave talents to be used, not buried. Creativity is available to anyone of any age.

If you visit my study, you'll see hanging on the wall an oil painting of a crippled boy holding a spotted terrier dog. The picture was painted by a woman who took up art after she was sixty years of age. No requirement kept her from painting during earlier years—she just didn't get around to it. I'm glad she started when she did.

Maybe creativity for you would be building something out of wood or brick. It could be expressing yourself in music. It might be weaving or sewing something in the old-style craftsmanship of past centuries. Whatever creativity means to you, give some thought to developing it.

You don't have to be educated to be creative. Grandma Moses produced primitive paintings for the fun of it. She made a fortune and proved that art school was no necessity for her. Some very productive people in the literary world have never been to college. The developer of the Polaroid Land Camera dropped out of Harvard University to begin a fabulous career of marketing his ideas.

You don't have to have ten talents. Creativity is not limited to the elite or the few exceptionally gifted. Some students whose IQ scores show the most potential actually flunk out in ordinary courses because they aren't motivated. Some of the most gifted people, similarly, once they're out of school, have hang-ups that keep them from producing. Creativity isn't limited to a few. Anyone can create something. It may not be a masterpiece in marble, but it could be a funny conversation piece made from matchsticks.

I believe the Creator of the universe has given every person a desire to create something. Creativity is a divinely given spark that can be fanned into a flame. It comes from God.

Some senior adults are unhappy and sad because they don't know how to express their creativity. They feel stifled and frustrated. If someone complained to me about "time on my hands," I would tell that person to go into a hobby and craft store. "Just take a look," I'd say, "at all the opportunities to make interesting and beautiful things."

Creativity is catching. At a senior adult Chautauqua at Ridgecrest, North Carolina, nine hundred people of varying talents studied and played together. Some who had given up any idea of doing something creative were turned on by the live wire people they met. At a talent show, a man who had taken up karate after the age of sixty gave a demonstration. A group of senior citizens from Lynchburg, Virginia, called the Ageless Wonders, presented a musical program in costume. A ninety-four-year-old man sang "I'd Rather Have Jesus." What happened after the applause died down and the audience left?

Hundreds of people were inspired to go home and do more. Some began to write stories and articles. Others began to sing. A few made puppets or worked in religious drama. Others decorated ceramic pieces or wove materials or carved. They had expressed their creativity.

Some people like to take up a craft just to have the feeling of mastering something new and fairly difficult like a person who wants to complete a difficult jigsaw puzzle. Nothing wrong about that.

Others want to take up a new craft in order to make some decorative pieces for the house or for gifts to friends at the holiday season.

Some take up a new venture that proves rather expensive, and they begin to sell their wares in order to pay for the raw materials. Through hobbies, some senior adults have discovered second vocations.

A man in Dunedin, Florida, Elbert Waterson, retired from the printing business and bought an addressing machine. He handles mailing lists for a newspaper and for other businesses. His hobby has become a full-time business.

A woman who began as a volunteer serving a church supper soon found herself employed every day in the big church kitchen, planning and supervising the many meals that were needed there.

Many people have gone into the amusing but expensive hobby of collecting things—from old Coca-Cola bottles to comic books. In flea markets, they're finding opportunities to swap, buy, and sell. Stamp and coin collections have become quite valuable, as any knowledgeable thief can tell you. But both these collections require study. As a person learns about stamps, a new world of geography opens up. As a person studies about coins, many facts from history come showering down to entertain and instruct.

You can learn about a hobby by reading about it. A better way is to ask someone in that hobby to explain it to you. Most hobbyists become as enthusiastic as evangelists when they tell about their special interest. I once asked a man about his orchid collection, and before long he was giving me offshoots and divided plants. I still have those orchids Frank Weeks gave me.

Another way is to visit or join a club that the people in that hobby have organized. In these clubs people are eager to share insights. You can find many kinds of clubs—from camellia growing to CB radio operating.

Before you start any hobby, you need to consider the time and the money it will require. After you get started, you'll find it hard to back out because of the expense. But when you face the financial part in advance, you can choose a hobby that is financially possible for you.

The Fascination of Touring

Another question in the same survey of Chautauqua attendants was on the one thing they had always wanted to do (provided they had the money). The largest group reported they wanted to travel. Travel in the United States was the answer of 25.6 percent, and travel to the Holy Land of 17.8 percent. The persons who answered this question reflected the wanderlust that many older persons feel. The respondents certainly didn't fit into the stereotype of the older person who wants to sit at home, never venturing out of the confines of familiar surroundings.

My mother-in-love, Nell Roeder Lipham, accompanied my wife, my daughter, and me to Europe recently. At the age of seventy-five she was willing to leave her familiar surroundings in Jackson, Mississippi, to travel to Italy, Germany, Austria, and Switzerland. She loved the trip. She abided by the first rule of international travelers: Don't fuss about customs and foods being different. After all, that was why she left home—to experience the unusual. And she didn't complain but enjoyed the new experiences. Her only regret was that she had listened to the advice of people over the years who had told her to see America first. She wished that she had gone to Europe earlier.

Senior adults find travel fascinating. When their traveling is with a like-minded group and for an uplifting purpose, they really love it. The Nazarene International Retreats of Golden Agers have reached hundreds of people since they started in 1973. They sometimes use the retreat facilities of the Presbyterians in Montreat, North Carolina, or of the Baptists at Glorieta, New Mexico. The Golden Agers come together in a beautiful setting for a time of spiritual enrichment, fellowship, crafts, and touring. The participants return home with a new feeling of the importance of their elder gifts.

Part of the fun of attending a senior adult conference is the travel there with other like-minded people. A bunch of older people board a bus as strangers but arrive at their destination as friends. They admit that part of the joy of travel is getting to know other people.

The American Association of Retired Persons operates dozens of tours each year. In the last five years travel on these AARP-sponsored tours has jumped by 400 percent. These include international travel. During the first three months of 1977, the dollar volume for travel to Europe exceeded the total for the entire previous year. Older travelers are raring to go.

Lots of senior citizens have heeded the slogan "Travel by bus and leave the driving to us." They have discovered the unlimited pass, such as the fifteen-day pass for $165. Others choose escorted tours to a picturesque or historic section of the country. On the escorted tours, participants know that hotel reservations, luggage handling, and other decisions about traveling will be handled by the tour director. I enjoyed such a tour in 1977 to see the Treasures of Tutankhamen at New Orleans. Most of the passengers were senior adults.

Another way to travel is by chartered bus. A church group or a club decides to go somewhere and charters a bus to take them to their destination and back home. I know some churches who own their own buses for local travel but depend on the luxury of the chartered liners for longer trips.

People who travel enlarge the world of their knowledge. They discover the depth of the Jordan where Jesus was baptized. They know the perfection of Michelangelo's Pieta in marble or the funerary mask of King Tut in gold. They taste the flavors of a meal on Fisherman's

Wharf in San Francisco or in the French Quarter of New Orleans. They can store the memory of a sunset over Waikiki Beach or a moment of meditation in the garden of Gethsemane. They can store up memories of the mist that hit their faces at Niagara Falls or the feel of total darkness in Mammoth Cave. They can feel a closeness with Paul when they walk down the streets of ancient Corinth or with Spurgeon when they visit his London Tabernacle. The feelings and memories of travel can never be duplicated by reading a book or by seeing someone else's slides. Travel is a unique contact with truth and beauty—a personal kind of experience that cannot permit a proxy.

Adventure

Beyond the thrill of mere traveling, you have no doubt discovered the underlying spirit of adventure. This word implies the encountering of risks. You see, adventure is a mind-set, a way of looking at life. The person with an adventuresome spirit never sees life as monotonous but as a series of fascinating events.

I met a retired couple who had come to North Carolina for a conference. They had driven from Texas in a big, comfortable car on the expressways. But when they reached the North Carolina border they felt the siren call of adventure. They left the expressway and took a small country road.

Nothing shocking happened to them. But they enjoyed the magnificence of the woods just before the leaves changed colors in the fall. And they stopped in an old-fashioned country store. They didn't know that such stores still existed, but they enjoyed a chance to meet some authentic mountaineers. They bought a slice of rat cheese before they left and nibbled on it as they resumed their trip. Those people had learned the success of adventurous living—leave the main highways and discover forgotten people and places.

The person who understands adventure has a good time, regardless of the place. A friend of mine who is an only child lost his father recently by a sudden heart attack. I called to give him my condolences. He asked if I knew how his father had died. He reported, with some satisfaction, that his father was coming out of the stadium after a football game when he was stricken. "Can you think of a better time to die," he asked, "than when you have been to the final game of the season—seeing Ole Miss and Mississippi State play, and seeing your team win? Isn't that a wonderful way to spend your last hours?"

How would you have answered? No doubt, you would have sensed that the bereaved son received some comfort in knowing that his dad, a faithful Christian, had maintained the spirit of adventure up to the end.

I know of a similar case. One of the regular senior adults in my Sunday School department was Stirton Oman, a successful contractor who had just completed a portion of the Alaska pipeline. He went with his children and grandchildren to the Bahamas for a vacation. In that beautiful spot, surrounded by the people he loved most, he died. Whether on construction jobs in Alaska or Pakistan or overseeing the installation of a septic tank at his church (one of the last things he did), Stirton lived a life of adventure.

I sense this same kind of attitude in the apostle Paul. He was willing to take risks, and he always wanted to travel to a new place to share his testimony of Christ's power in his life.

"But now having no more place in these parts, and having a great desire these many years to come unto you; Whensoever I take my journey into Spain, I will come to you: for I trust to see you in my journey, and to be brought on my way thitherward by you, if first I be somewhat filled with your company" (Rom. 15:23–24).

The noted philosopher Alfred North Whitehead said, "Without adventure, civilization is in full decay." I propose a similar statement, changing only one word: "Without adventure, self is in full decay."

Laziness and inertia can smother the spirit of adventure unless you are careful. Some senior adults I know quit going to concerts and parties, saying, "They're just not worth the trouble." Some widows I know say, "I don't get out at night anymore. I'm afraid to come back to an empty house." These poor souls are missing out on some unique opportunities to be with others and to enrich their lives. Actually some of them are like the farmer who does the same thing all the time; he plows down the same furrow. If he keeps on in the same furrow, he'll find himself in a rut. And you know a rut is simply a grave with the ends extended. So I would encourage you to stir up the fires of adventure, and get out of that rut.

You can practice the art of adventure when you break the chain of routine. Take up something new and different. I'm not talking about round-the-world trips. Maybe just going across town would be fun. None of the senior adults I know go to movies, saying that Hollywood producers don't make them like they used to and they can see the same thing in a few years on TV. It might be an adventure for you to attend a film and see how nice it is to see a picture without interruptions for commercials. But more than that, imagine the fun of discussing the picture with a teenager.

One of the nicest trips my wife and I ever made was not to a distant place—it was right here in our own state of Tennessee. We went to Reelfoot Lake—an unusual geographical feature that had been formed by the great earthquakes of 1812 and 1813. The cypress knees there look like a Louisiana bayou. But we went for a purpose more adventuresome than just looking at the beautiful swampy lake. We went in early January for an eagle watch. I saw more American bald eagles wintering there than I had seen in the rest of my life put together. I enjoyed the adventure of meeting new people who had been drawn to that place for the common purpose of observing the majestic bird that symbolizes our country.

When you see a ship in a harbor, you know that it's safe there. But then remember that a ship was built to sail out into the expanse of the blue oceans. A life is like that ship—the more cautious that life is, the less opportunity it has for adventure.

Keep your eyes open for adventure. Listen to the siren sounds that call you from the humdrum. Feel the winds that blow mysteriously from one unknown part of the globe to another. Taste the exotic foods that other peoples have discovered and praised. Smell the perfumes of far-away places. Surely, the adventuresome spirit is a gift from the Creator.

Stella has the right idea. She's willing to try new activities. On her ninety-sixth birthday she went on a motorcycle ride. People all over Mount Sterling, Illinois, where she lives in a retirement home, were delighted to see her zoom past. But they weren't too surprised. The previous year, on her ninety-fifth birthday, she had taken an airplane ride. Already Stella is trying to think of something different for her ninety-seventh celebration. Since she has never been married, she's giving some thought to matrimony. (Maybe she'll settle for a skateboard ride—it might be less complicated.) But I salute Stella Dennis—a woman who hasn't lost the spirit of adventure. She's curious. She's alive. She's still growing.

I've heard of some groups that are exceptional. There's a swimming team of senior adults in Arizona and another one in Hawaii. A group in Fort Pierce, Florida, called the "Galloping Grannies" is a chorus line of fourteen women, ranging in age from sixty-one to seventy-six. I always enjoy seeing the "Ageless Wonders," a group of entertainers from Lynchburg, Virginia; they sing, recite, and tell tall tales.

When older persons form such a group, they accomplish at least two things. They have a wonderful time performing with other senior citizens. They contradict public stereotypes of aging people withdrawing from activities and fun. The senior adult who exercises alone, travels, or joins a group of like-minded people is enlarging a world that will keep on expanding.

8
Be a Lifelong Learner

Some people expend great amounts of money and energy on their bodies and forget about their brains. Like the body, the brain needs exercise to function efficiently.

Senior adults who want to enlarge their worlds have the marvelous opportunity of using their minds. I'd like to encourage every person who reads this book to become a lifelong learner. I'd like to know that the reader will move on from this book to something more difficult. I'd like to think that I had influenced one person to return to a college campus to take a course that opened new doors of inspiration.

You can be a lifelong learner if you continue to study and learn. The easiest place to begin is to attend a Sunday School class. There with others you can seek and discuss meaning in the passage that is spotlighted. Of course, you could study your Bible at home by yourself; but when you hear the questions and comments of a teacher and other members of your class, you will be stimulated to think. What if someone disagrees with you? Wonderful. That disagreement will help you get your own thoughts in perspective. So when somebody comes up with a different interpretation from your own, listen carefully. Think through your own position. Explain how you arrived at your conclusion.

You can make your Sunday School experience a more meaningful one. Ask yourself, *What am I putting into this learning experience?* Then compare what you would be doing if you were taking the same lessons for credit in a college course on Bible.

You'd see several differences between your casual approach to Sunday School and a college student's approach to a class. You'd see a new meaning to study. How can you call it study when you merely glance over the lesson materials late on a Saturday night or while someone is driving you to church on Sunday morning? If you were taking a course on a college campus you would be expected to study. You'd be expected to do some parallel reading. Well, my friend, you could do both of those activities for your Sunday School class—and when you do, I'll guarantee you'll get a lot more from the class.

Some Sunday School teachers give special assignments and expect reports, but I don't know any who give grades. Of course, some teachers give a pretest before a unit of study, and the student can use this test to see what he or she needs to study the most. Then a posttest helps to see the amount of improvement. Not many teachers offer tests, but they can serve a valuable purpose of showing Bible students just where they are in their development.

Start with Sunday School, but don't stop there. Consider some other kinds of study.

Pearly Gray Matter

The brain is subject to the pearl principle. Just as a little irritation in the oyster produces a pearl, so a problem can become a jewel in your mind. Exercising your brain with a problem can keep you from growing "old" (in the bad sense).

Educators and scientists point to the ideas of resistance and persistence. They agree that the best mental exercise is that in which you have to deal with resistance. Like isometric exercises for the body, difficult tasks help the mind. Problem solving is a gift—thank God for it.

Like the experience of jogging, a tiny bit of mental exercise doesn't help much—you have to do a lot of it and keep at it. In a cerebral workout, persistence brings rewards. Researchers say that working a crossword puzzle once in a while doesn't help much, but if you daily are dealing with a retarded child, teaching an international student English, or building a complicated piece of furniture, the mental rewards are better.

How can you stick with it? Challenge yourself to keep on until you get your mental second breath; then persist until you win. You'll be less likely to quit if you're helping someone who expects you or if you're receiving money for a job—then you will be more likely to continue without quitting.

Although the idea of continuing education isn't new, it presents one of the great areas for senior progress. College and vocational courses have been available for some time, but few senior adults are taking advantage

of them. Look at the figures compiled by Louis Harris
and Associates, Inc., for the National Council on the Aging, Inc. Only 2 percent of those over sixty-five were
enrolled in an educational institution or enrolled in a
course. Of that number, the largest group was taking a
course at a church—26 percent. Next, 24 percent were
enrolled in a college or university, and 19 percent were
taking a course in an adult education school.

For the adult educator, the fields are white unto harvest. Most Christians have always believed in adult education. Never have our Sunday Schools issued any sort of
graduation diploma to teenagers or given them the impression that they had completed their religious education. On the contrary, Sunday Schools have been closely
graded to provide a class for every age group in the
church. This environment—this ambience should make
every church the primary place that a senior adult could
turn to for courses in church history, doctrine, and biblical
interpretation. We used to have study courses that were
widely attended, but the pendulum has swung. Now that
secular education is discovering what we have known
all the time—that adults can learn—maybe churches will
again offer study courses. I'm not talking about Mickey
Mouse stuff; I mean classes on a college level. Classes
that will challenge and inspire. There are thousands of
senior adults who don't want to be spoonfed. They want
to chew on the meatier matters of their faith for themselves.

What are the reasons elders are enrolled in courses?
Most give these answers in this order: to expand my
knowledge about a field or hobby, to make good use of

my time, and to be with other people. They're worthy reasons, aren't they? The church can provide for its senior adults who have similar needs and desires. You might ask whether such an undertaking is really possible. Sure.

Opportunities for Study

Although you might have thought about these, I want to mention several types of opportunities: study by correspondence from Nashville, a model interdenominational center in Kansas City, and college or night school.

Study by correspondence. Many people who pick up a book for enrichment and growth feel the need for some guidance. They want help with it. They'd even be willing to take a test on it to get some feedback. They want to know how they're doing.

Adult education emphasizes the use of feedback to correct, to reinforce, and to motivate. The correspondence course offers this kind of tutoring. Many courses are available—some you might hear about over radio or TV seem to be schemes to get you on some evangelist's sucker list. Not so with anything offered by a reliable group of churches or denomination by which money is kept to a minimum and learning to a maximum.

One of the first systems that many senior adults have discovered is the Home Study Institute of the Seminary Extension Department, Southern Baptist Convention. The Institute offers approximately forty college-level correspondence courses in biblical, theological, historical, and practical subject areas. These courses are available to any adult church member seeking academically oriented learning opportunities.

When you enroll in a correspondence course with the Home Study Institute, you receive a textbook, a study guide, and a correspondence kit—all for a nominal fee. You'll get lesson materials organized by units of study. When you complete a unit of study, you mail the unit examination to the Institute for correction, grading, comment, and subject matter guidance by a qualified instructor. All of the Institute's instructors have master's or doctor's degrees in the subject areas they instruct.

From this interchange a student-teacher relationship develops—like pen pals raised to a higher level. When you study by correspondence with the Home Study Institute, you're being tutored by mail.

In this program of home study, you can choose your goal and work toward it. Select one of several specialization certificates: Educational, Pastoral Ministries, or Advanced. Imagine the satisfaction of taking enough courses to earn one of these to hang on your den wall. One woman in Pass Christian, Mississippi, has done this and would recommend that you do the same. She is Allie Lee Wharton. This lifelong learner isn't a person who does nothing else. She's organist, choir director, and director of a children's department in her church. Yet she still has taken time to complete sixteen courses for a diploma and is working on an advanced diploma.

If you want to find out more about this marvelous opportunity for correspondence study, just write for a free curriculum guide that describes the courses and get an application form. Here is the address: Seminary Extension Home Study Institute, Southern Baptist Convention

Building, 460 James Robertson Parkway, Nashville, Tennessee 37219.

Another correspondence course available is tied in with a popular type TV show. It is jointly produced by the Sunday School Board and the Radio and Television Commission of the Southern Baptist Convention and is offered on selected stations around the country. Pitched on a lower academic level, with less teacher-student contact, the course is available to anyone who writes in. Units of study lasting for four or five weeks will include the following topics: the nature of God, the nature of mankind, the meaning of salvation, loneliness, the Holy Spirit, the future, Christian growth, and so forth. Senior adults would not have to watch the TV shows to take the course, but they would get maximum benefit from doing both. The course is free of charge, but users are invited to make a contribution.

For more information on this popular, simplified course, write Home Bible Study Ministries, Nashville, Tennessee 37234.

If you're interested in a free, simple guide to a book-by-book study of the Bible and don't want to bother with mailing in tests, write for information: Correspondence Bible Course, Home Mission Board of the Southern Baptist Convention, 1350 Spring Street, N. W., Atlanta, Georgia 30309. This course has been in existence for over thirty years, and 100,000 students have enrolled during these years.

A Model Interdenominational Learning Center. Twenty-two churches and synagogues in the Country Club-Waldo section of Kansas City cooperate to run The

Shepherd's Center, 5218 Oak Street, Kansas City, Missouri 64112. That organization's purpose is to help older persons find more meaningful lives.

One of the most exciting activities of the center, located in the facilities of a United Methodist Church, is called Adventures in Learning. Each Friday, from 9:00 A.M. to 3:00 P.M., more than thirty classes and activities are offered by volunteer instructors. (None are paid.) Students arrive early, keyed up and ready to learn. They choose from such courses as international relations, foreign languages, travelogues, Bible courses, personal growth, estate planning, book reviews, art history, gardening, music, grooming for older persons, yoga, and similar subjects. Classes are held eleven months of the year.

Senior adults enroll with a $2.50 fee each term, and they can take as many courses as they can fit into the allotted hours. A forum at noon offers variety from the other scheduled courses; it features musical entertainment and talks by community leaders. A hot lunch is served for a nominal fee. Those who prefer bring a sack lunch.

This learning approach was built on the model that has been used successfully for fifteen years by St. Luke's United Methodist Church, 1506 North Harvey Street, Oklahoma City, Oklahoma 73103.

Adult education has many side effects that you might not expect. I know a woman in her seventies who had been a nurse and who returned to Duke University to get her master's degree in nursing. One of the unexpected pleasures for her was to get to know the younger students and try to influence them toward a Christian philosophy of nursing.

What They Don't Know Can Hurt Them

In several places where I have spoken, I have asked how many people were enrolled in some adult course at a college or vocational school. Few said they were, and I tried to decide the reasons so many senior citizens don't go back to college classes.

1. They don't know of the availability of classes to them. The institutions that offer these courses need to do a much better job with public relations. States that offer tuition-free courses should use every source possible to get out the news. All the media, if given a chance, would offer free coverage to announcements and would feature interviews with senior adults who have returned to the campus.

2. They don't know anybody who has gone. They need models. They will respond to people who have tried it and liked it. They want to hear someone talk enthusiastically about the experience before they take the plunge into the supposedly cold waters of academic life. If they met a senior adult student in person, they would be more willing to listen to that person's ideas. If, however, they only had the opportunity of seeing that person interviewed on TV or heard that person on a radio talk show or read about that senior student in an article, they would still feel positively about the program of continuing education.

3. They associate the classroom with unpleasant experi-

ences in the past. They recall dull lectures and rote exercises. They remember times in which they were called on to recite and were humiliated in front of their peers. They fear a repetition of that trauma before a classroom of sophisticated college students.

4. They don't want to be the only senior adult in the class. Conversely, many don't want to be in a class comprised of senior citizens only. Some would prefer a mix of young and old.

5. They are unwilling to try something new. Studies show that the ones most interested in taking a course on the college level are ones who have already had some college work. Others are afraid and are overly cautious. Actually, they don't know what they're missing.

6. They have thought of college courses as preparation for a vocation, not as an end in themselves. They need a new view of enrichment and pleasure that they derive from a learning experience.

7. They have accepted the stereotype that older people can't learn. Many tests in the past few decades have proven that senior adults can learn. In some procedures, the older persons take longer in doing a task or in learning a fact. But they hold on to what they have learned sometimes better than the younger students dealing with new facts. The senior adults have a framework of experience into which they can fit the new material.

What senior adults don't know about continuing education can hurt them—depriving them of opportunities of enlarging their world. Therefore, college administrations and faculties, together with other senior adult leaders, have a big task. Clubs need speakers. Newspapers and radio/TV talk shows are always looking for a new angle. An older student who is enthusiastic could fill the bill on any of these openings.

Maybe in the future, the word about courses for older persons will spread. Friends can share insights with one another. Perhaps institutions can offer incentives other than free tuition. The possibilities for continuing education are exciting.

I believe that Christian leaders have a selling job to do in the field of continuing education. When the Harris pollsters asked older people why they weren't taking a course, 27 percent replied that they were too old, and 7 percent didn't know of any courses available.

Senior adults who have taken a course could tell their friends. They could write a letter to a newspaper editor or call in to a radio or TV talk show and relate the thrill of going to school with students of a younger generation.

Some widows I know say they would be interested only if the courses were offered in the daytime. But if several widows got together in a car pool, they would have a grand time going to and from the campus. Or they could ask a young man to escort them (either as a voluntary act or for pay). If they really want to learn, they'll find a way to get past the excuses.

Senior adult friend, what if your hindsight of today had been your foresight of yesterday? What would you have done differently if you could have known when you were younger what life would be like today? Some people were asked this question. Most of them responded in the financial realm. They would have given more attention to saving money and making the right investments to draw dividends in their old age. Maybe that is the way you would respond. But consider another response.

A smaller group expressed a wish that they had received more eduction. A significant statement! And a very different statement from the first.

Is it too late to acquire more of each—money and education? With money, you would find it almost impossible now to make an investment large enough to benefit you. With education the picture is reversed. You can start at any time. You can begin receiving dividends immediately.

I get a thrill out of reading or hearing about an oldster who has returned to the campus. Consider a few of these. An eighty-nine-year-old man is studying for his doctorate in American history at Tallahassee, Florida. A ninety-year-old man is studying French at Duke University. A ninety-nine-year-old student is enrolled at Delta College in Michigan. Also in Michigan, a sixty-two-year-old woman attends a yoga class along with her mother, age ninety-two.

Some high schools are open at night to teach senior adults everything from accounting to zoology, from furniture upholstering to bookkeeping. Many community colleges open their doors to any senior adult who would like to attend regular classes. More than half the state university systems offer free tuition to older Americans who want to audit the classes in a nondegree program.

Anytime a senior adult signs up to attend a conference center, a senior adult Chautauqua, that person is enlarging the world of the mind. If no classes are available, there's always the possibility of correspondence courses. Many are offered by denominational headquarters.

9
Make an Impact on Your Family and Friends

I'm tired of seeing books on how to manipulate people—to get them to do what you want them to do for you. I don't want this chapter title to mislead you into thinking this is one of those books.

I'm interested in the impact you can make because your heart is so filled with Christian love that people will feel its throbbing when they come near you. I'm talking about genuine concern.

What about your influence on your own family? It's harder to give a Christian witness to your own family than to anyone else. Why? Because family members can spot any inconsistency. They'll cry "Phony" or else turn you off. So most people don't say anything to offend close relatives about matters of faith and practice. They have an uneasy truce going.

A Life Review

I want to urge you to enlarge your world by making a conscious effort to influence your family in God's direction. Take those grandchildren, for instance. So what if they're teenagers? You still speak the same language— almost. Try adding the vocabulary of love. Show an interest in their interests. I'll bet they'll respond.

My Aunt Ella Kate, now in her eighties, lives in California with her daughter's family. She has heard so many of her older friends recite boring accounts of the past that she has stopped talking about the old days. These are two extremes. I told her to hit a happy medium with me and tell me a little about what my grandfather was like (since he died before I was born).

Gerontologists have discovered a technique that really works with most senior adults—a life review. This procedure gives the senior adult an audience and raises the elder's sense of self-worth.

Some older people, like Aunt Ella Kate, have refrained from talking about their earlier life, afraid they would create barriers of distance with younger people. They don't want to be laughed at or walked out on by teenagers.

The life review can change all that. The older person can make the life review an occasion. He or she can suggest to the teenager, "I can put some things on your tape recorder if you need them for a history class or for your own interest. I can tell you the games we used to play." If the younger set never seems interested, you can whet their appetite. You can say, "I can tell you what people wore before World War I—or about the first women who worked or about the first automobile I ever saw."

You might want to set a time to do it. This would add to the teenager's anticipation of the event. It would give you time to get your thoughts organized so that you wouldn't ramble and waste another's time.

I interviewed my parents and my mother-in-love. I

learned things about all three of them I hadn't heard before—not because they weren't willing to tell me but because they weren't sure I was interested. A tape-recorded interview symbolized my concern. I learned the importance and influence of teachers and preachers in their lives. I learned about their first jobs and how they saved money.

You can pass along some insights to your children and grandchildren. You will of course, be careful of boring them or preaching to them. If you share your happinesses and sorrows with them, they will respond to your love.

Leave a Legacy

Have you ever had something passed along to you from a previous generation? My friend Ruby Hankins has a stereoscope mounted on a table that belonged to her grandfather, along with six hundred photos from around the world. Another friend owns a Lincoln-type bed on which her grandmother gave birth to all her children. My friend Hank has the blacksmith tools that belonged to one grandfather and a sprinkle-type blotter from the other—a circuit-riding Methodist preacher.

Senior adults need to realize the importance of passing something important along. One of the most appealing poems ever to appear in *Mature Living* was by ninety-year-old Bess Foster Smith:

> I want a checkered tablecloth
>   Upon my kitchen table,
> A scarlet rose geranium
>   Within my window gable.

I want a rug made of rags
  Upon my kitchen floor,
A motto card, "God Bless Our Home"
  To hang above the door.

A whatnot in the corner
  To hold some treasured things,
A row of feathered fishing lures
  And a pink seashell that sings.

These were the things at Grandma's house
  By which I was beguiled—
Now they are precious memories
  I wish for my grandchild.[1]

A tradition is something you pass along. Maybe you
have something that you have never thought of as a part
of tradition. Maybe you have some skill you could pass
along to a grandchild or even to a stranger. Wouldn't it
be a waste of money to have a hundred-dollar bill buried
in a coffin with you—no one could get any benefit from
the money. An even worse waste is to carry some old
craft or skill to the grave with you. Some high school
girl would like to learn tatting from you; some teenage
boy would enjoy learning how to shoe a horse. If your
own relatives or neighbors aren't interested in learning
these and other skills, you can pass them along to strangers. Get a high school teacher to announce in a home
economics class about the tatting or an industrial arts
teacher to tell about the horseshoeing. Likely they will
find volunteers to learn from you.

Of course, the main legacy you can leave your children,
grandchildren, or great-grandchildren is your special approach to the Christian way. As you have walked along
the path these many decades, you've seen some mean-

ingful sights. You've learned to avoid some rough places in the road. You can pass along these insights—your Christian life-style. Isn't that the greatest gift you could bequeath?

Two people were talking about a rich man who had just died. One asked, "What did he leave?"

"Everything. He left everything," was the answer.

What will you leave behind? Most people think about money, but I'd like for you to think of how that money will be used. More important, I wish you'd think of leaving parts of your body.

One of the saddest sights in the town of Clayton, North Carolina, was a two-story white frame house that was deteriorating. The story people told was that it had been left to some sisters who couldn't agree on who would live in it—so none of them did. And the house was falling apart.

You can leave behind an influence as negative as that house. Or you can leave behind a happy philosophy like the poem about the tablecloth and the fishing lures.

I know of a woman in Mississippi, Mrs. Winona Odle Ice, who went blind at the age of seventy-nine. She didn't give up. She learned to read Braille and used a talking-book service to keep up with magazines and books.

Ten years later, her doctor told her she should try a cornea transplant. One night she was called to the University of Mississippi Hospital, where an anonymous male accident victim had donated his eyes. Four days later she could see.

She said the experience was like being born again. At eighty-nine, she started reading the Bible through. She now types her own letters, watches TV, and takes a deeper interest in people's needs. Mrs. Ice received something that someone left her—the cornea of two healthy eyeballs. What a gift!

You might do the same thing with a gift of a part of your body. Or you might give a gift of your philosophy expressed in a poem, a letter, a book, or a recording.

A newspaper reporter in Washington asked his Georgia father what he'd done that he was proud of. The older man answered, "I've turned in three fire alarms, none false." Isn't that a marvelous statement of modesty and integrity? That man left something more valuable to his son than a large estate; his son shared these cherished words with readers across the United States.

Memories that Bless

The finest, most advanced computer in the world is the human brain. One of the most complicated activities of this computer is the process of recall. You and I refer to it as remembering. You can file away facts and attitudes for years. You think they're forgotten or lost. Then something happens: the smell of baking gingerbread, the touch of a snowball, the sight of a man wearing a cap like the one the school bully wore, or the sounds of "Nearer, My God, to Thee." These sensations have triggered long-lost hostilities or feelings of devotion.

That's a part of the marvelous gift of memory.

You can misuse memory. You can let it ruin your present. Take persons with happy pasts; they can reminisce about the good old days and almost forget the present. They can fly from present reality on wings of memory.

This is what Job did at one point in his struggle for patience. The diseased, tortured man, without a family, said, "Oh that I were as in months past, as in the days when God preserved me" (Job 29:2).

He turned his mind back to the days of his youth (v. 4). The word he used for youth meant to pick fruit; it was a harvesttime—a period of joy and plenty. A simple recalling of this prosperity should have brought him enjoyment, but it didn't. His wish for the good old days made him miserable in the bad new days. On the cake of sadness, he added a topping of bitterness. On many occasions, he acted in an exemplary way; at this time, however, he demonstrated a way you and I can abuse our memories.

Another way you can misuse memory is to become chained to the past. You can build up guilt feelings about events in the past, but these feelings do not alter the facts or change the past. They simply make you more miserable. The writer of the Rubaiyat captured this fact:

> The Moving Finger writes; and, having writ,
> Moves on: nor all your Piety nor Wit
> Shall lure it back to cancel half a Line
> Nor all your Tears wash out a Word of it.

The words are true. You can't change your memories. What can you do? Change your attitude toward them. Sometimes Christians feel that God has forgiven them, but they can't forgive themselves. Perhaps they need to pour out their distress to a trusted Christian counselor— either a professional or a lay counselor.

Do you take seriously some foolish mistakes you made years ago? For instance, some adolescent anger or some

childish theft? Perhaps you need to take out your childhood memories and laugh at them. If God can forgive
these trivialities, certainly you can get a new attitude
toward them. Like the apostle Paul, you can forget those
things which are behind. (See Phil. 3:13.)

Use your memories to bless your life now. You have
been feeding information into that computer of yours
for years. Now it can work for you. Punch the print-out
button, and let it deliver the best recollections from your
past. Enjoy the blessings of memory. Recall an old song
or a past event.

In the early stages of planning the magazine *Mature
Living,* Lee Sizemore suggested a regular feature called
"I Remember When . . . " I agreed that senior adult
readers would enjoy some nostalgia. Many people have
commented on how much they enjoy this section of the
magazine. And free-lance writers contribute more articles to this section than to any other department of
Mature Living except poetry.

But note that the magazine carries only a couple of
pages of nostalgia. Memories are a lot like perfume—nice
if sniffed in small amounts but dangerous if swallowed.
So I advise a little nostalgia, but I warn against escaping
into a dream world.

You can find guidance for your present by reviewing
the past. Before you reached these golden years, you
worked out a way of life with God's help. You tried it
out. You embellished it with a system of beliefs and a
style of action. Now you can simplify it by trimming off
the excess, majoring on the essentials. These present years
can be happier because of your correct use of the past.

These memories can guide your present. Regardless of whether they are pleasant or unpleasant, they can be used as research material, a backlog of experience. Instead of binding you to them and blinding you to life, they can free you to act and to think as a responsible believer.

Some people worry themselves sick over their health. Do you? Past regrets could sour your spirit. Toss them out. Be thankful.

Don't worry when your memory occasionally slips. This happens to everybody. It can be a blessing. You don't need to keep your marvelous memory machine stuffed with a lot of nonusable facts—like the number of all your old car license tags, the telephone numbers of people in other towns, the teams who played in past World Series games, and similar items. Forget them. If you really need some information, just call up the courthouse or the library.

You have a wonderful excuse if you forget a bothersome committee meeting or a sensitive friend's birthday. Laugh and say, "I must be getting old; it just slipped my mind."

Your memory computer has filed away in its safest section those Scripture verses you learned in your early years. A blind lady in her nineties once said to me, "I am grateful for the Scriptures that I learned when my mind was young and my eyes were bright. I wish I had learned more. They bless my life today."

Wise and inspired was the psalmist who said, "Thy word have I hid in mine heart, that I might not sin against thee" (Ps. 119:11).

Helping Others Know the Past

Let me remind you of one of the most negative symbolic acts of our time; it shows one attitude toward the past. It happened in Rome. A thirty-three-year-old man, Laszlo Toth, slithered out of the touring crowds in St. Peter's Basilica. He climbed the balustrade up to Michelangelo's delicate sculpture, the Pieta. He didn't pause to admire the artistry of the only signed sculpture by the world's foremost sculptor. He didn't meditate on the emotions of Mary holding the lifeless form of the crucified Jesus. Instead, the vandal with a hammer began pounding away at the lifelike masterpiece. As he chipped off splintered pieces, Toth screamed, "I am Jesus Christ!" By the time guards restrained him, he had damaged the priceless work that a twenty-four-year-old genius had completed some 475 years before.

If you have been in Rome in recent months, you know that the masterpiece has been restored and placed behind bulletproof glass. Even though you couldn't see a single line or crack, you still felt: What a shame! This isn't the way Michelangelo left it. A deranged person has tampered with the marvelous masterpiece.

His destructive act symbolizes the belligerent mood of many around the world. Some revolutionaries want to throw away everything from the past. Others, not quite as destructive, want to discard or retire all older ideas and principles.

At this point, you can have some input. The active senior adult can make an impression and help some younger person gain a perspective on the past. Here's how.

Admit that everything in the past wasn't perfect. Some practices by religious people, such as selling slaves, ostracizing sinners, and burning witches needed to be abandoned.

Just because something was simple or primitive doesn't mean that it was inferior. Recall for a young listener the older practices of education—the one-room schoolhouse, for instance. Project a quaint picture of it on the screen of your conversation. Tell about the carved desks with inkwells, the potbellied stove, the water bucket and dipper, the coal house, the privies, the teacher's bell, the McGuffey readers, the spelling bees, and the teacher's treat of hard candy at the end of the year. As antiquated as the details seem, they offer a fascinating glimpse to the modern young person. Furthermore, some of the old methods of education from that period are creeping back into modern pedagogy—nongraded classes and a return to the basics of reading, writing, and arithmetic.

You might also like to describe for some young friend or relative the old religious practices—the hour-long sermons, the all-day sings, the dinners on the grounds, the baptisms in the creek, Scripture memorizing contests, and the old songs, such as "Beulah Land," "The Church in the Wildwood," "When They Ring Those Golden Bells," and "Will There Be Any Stars in My Crown?" Such a picture of the past should interest the teenager. Also, you could point out the emphasis on morality and the feeling of fellowship in a small community of believers. These later ideas, whether you point them out or not, will be obvious to the young person.

Point out the value of unchanging truth. When people of the now generation think of the past, they are tempted to focus on primitive skills in medicine or horse-and-buggy transportation. Don't let them assume that because something is old, it is old-fashioned. Some people seem to believe that if something didn't happen in their lifetime and in their community, the event was unimportant.

In the field of faith and doctrine, you can look back to the Golden Age. Just as the artist looks back to the Renaissance, so can the religious educator look back to Jesus' teachings. The Master's teachings on the two great Commandments are as relevant to this age as the morning newspaper and as everlasting as the Father's love.

In the field of Christian teaching, the early church members needed the truth. They wanted to learn from apostles who had followed Jesus during his teaching and healing ministry and had seen him after he was raised from the dead. (See Acts 1:21–22.) The true teachings they passed along became a precious heritage. Recall that Paul told young Timothy, "Hold fast the form of sound words, which thou hast heard of me, in faith and love which is in Christ Jesus" (2 Tim. 1:13).

The senior adult today should keep up with all the changes that are happening. But the older person needs to distinguish between things that are abiding and those that are temporary.

The senior adult who is alert to opportunities for conversation can pass along to people of a younger generation something of a new appreciation of the past and its assets. Without being pushy, interested older persons can make themselves available to speak to school classes, Scout troops, and church youth groups. When Winnie Pearce let it be known that she had time to tell about her childhood in North Carolina's Appalachia, she began to receive numerous invitations. In the town of Buies Creek, where she and Winston Pearce have retired, the schoolteachers know they can count on her to enliven their classes with some anecdotes that are as reliable as the encyclopedia and as funny as Minnie Pearl's. She enjoys entertaining both the elementary school classes and the high school classes.

When I interviewed Art Linkletter in his Beverly Hills office, I asked him how he was able to relate so well to children. The star, who had just turned sixty-five, said, "There is a child in all of us. I let them see the child in me, and I appeal to the child in them. I am interested in them, and they can tell it." Any older person who keeps in mind the worth of the younger person will find contact and communication much easier.

A senior adult woman with beautiful white hair and a lovely complexion like satin, Ruth Neely, stood at a Thanksgiving service I attended. She said, "The pastor of the church at Franklin, Tennessee, called me recently and said the three most beautiful words in the language: 'We need you.'"

They needed her to help write a history of the church she had attended as a girl. She decided she would write the history in the form of a play that would appeal to young and old alike. But they gave this woman an opportunity to use her talents in God's work. She felt needed. The event occurred just after the death of her dear brother, and it helped her through some difficult days of bereavement. People need to feel needed.

A part of communication is tolerance. One benefit that

comes from travel is the respect that the older traveler develops for other nationalities' places of worship and for their distinctive ideas. This same tolerance needs some practice in your own church.

There's no need for you to throw a fit if your church's youth want to display a banner or two and play some loud music at a worship service. Don't major on the minor. Be a good sport. My friend Daisy Perry did her part at a Christmas banquet. In a skit about what gifts a person might receive, she came out in a hippie outfit, twirling a gold chain necklace. My former pastor, Gaye McGlothlen, a dignified man in his sixties, is well known for his bald head. In the same skit, he covered his glistening dome with a male wig and was almost unrecognizable. People, especially the youth, enjoyed the fact that senior adults could laugh at themselves.

Guard the best that comes from the past. Part of your responsibility is to protect unchanging truth. Guards must protect ancient works of art from vandalism and theft. You need to protect the church fellowship that you and others have worked to build. One gossiping member or a couple of chronic complainers can begin to wreck the work of years. I'm sure that the reader of this book would never destroy the masterpiece of fellowship. Don't let other careless people do it.

The best changes come gradually with study and preparation. Take a political party, a social institution, or a church—if any of these is unwilling to make changes, it leaves itself vulnerable to revolution. The resulting jolting changes are seldom beneficial.

The senior adults who are doing the most to enlarge their world seem to be the ones who recall the past and take the best from it. But they also live in the present, without any escapism in the direction of past or future. They are happy in the now.

Witnessing to Other Senior Adults

As you enlarge your world, you will discover that other senior adults are traveling a lonesome road and need some companionship. You have the marvelous opportunity of offering your Christian life-style to some sixty-year-old person who has never made a commitment to Christ as Savior.

Some people in Billings, Montana, were alert to the needs of a senior adult woman, Mrs. Bridges. They let her live with them while the water pipes at her home were frozen. They took her to church with them.

For two weeks, Mrs. Bridges recalled the invitation hymn she heard on her first visit to the church, "Just As I Am." She kept a lump in her throat until she responded to the invitation.

Senior adults who have never made life's greatest decision find great joy when they find the Savior. Perhaps someone you know is on the verge of deciding to accept Christ, and you could have a part in that commitment.

The traditional approach has been to use a hard sell to get another person to do something *you* decided was best. The way Jesus used was to help people decide what *they* felt was the most productive and meaningful decision.

The Layperson as Counselor

There are not enough professional counselors, chaplains, and psychiatrists to do all the work that needs to be done in healing personalities. Lay people can do this same work if they understand what they are doing.

The senior adult is tempted to underestimate the latent power in the helping relationship. One person said, "I don't know what to advise people." That's not it. You don't advise. You relate as a friend.

The person-on-the-street view sees the lay counselor as ineffective. It tends to discount the change that the suffering person can experience.

Recently the father of a young man in his twenties said to me, "I believe in miracles." This young man had been such a problem as a teenager that he had to be given psychiatric help. But now, through a combination of that help, the prayers of his parents, the patience of the young man's loving wife, and his determination to organize his life, he has changed. He is coping with life's problems.

You can also see miracles take place. Work with a friend. Don't give up. People can change. But think what causes that change: one or more relationships of trust. Almost like a marriage relation, two people make a covenant with each other to understand but to keep quiet about it. God works through this relationship of trust in order to work healing growth.

Use Your CB, Good Buddy

A fad as big as saddle oxfords and hula hoops is the citizen's band radio—the CB fad. But this fad, in contrast to many in the past, reaches an older audience. Many senior adults have equipped their cars with CB radios. Some have base stations in their homes. Occasionally, you hear a nickname on the CB radio that identifies an active Christian, such as "Child of the King" or "Sky Pilot."

Out in Claude, Texas, a shut-in named Tom Henry operates a base station. When a rancher is going to be late, he calls Tom, who relays the message to the rancher's wife by telephone. Tom keeps in touch with the emergencies and with the ordinary events in his community. He is a homebound person who has used his CB radio to break out of the boundaries of his room. He reaches out to others.

The radio offers senior adults a way to expand and enlarge their world. Some can use a ham radio to contact missionaries or to help missionaries keep in contact with their families. Others will choose the CB radio to make acquaintances in their travels. Any contact, however, offers a challenge to make an impact for God.

Visit the Homebound

People who are shut in often feel isolated. They yearn for a visit as a worker in the cotton fields yearns for a dipper of water. You can bring that refreshing change.

I know of a seventy-one-year-old man in Oklahoma City who likes to visit the homebound. He's a guy who never does things halfheartedly. He owns sixty suits. He has attended as many as eighty-seven basketball games in a six-week span. But best of all—are you ready?—he makes 150 or more visits to shut-ins every month. He is John M. Salvo, director of the Homebound Department, Trinity Baptist Church, Oklahoma City.

Anyone can visit a shut-in. All you need to remember

is to let your host or hostess talk. Show interest and love. If that homebound person really wants to hear what happened at the church social or really would like to know how you feel about denominational colleges, share your views. But don't dominate the conversation. Don't leave behind you any critical remarks or negative thoughts. If the person wants you to lead in prayer, do so before you leave. If you have been an interested and concerned listener, you have succeeded in your visit.

10
Involved in World Missions

No longer isolated in little corners of America, senior adults today feel a part of the world. Persons who watch the evening news on television know as much about Rhodesia as they do about West Virginia. They feel that they understand Anwar Sadat as well as they do their own senator.

Volunteer Missionaries

Senior adults could become missionaries. They have read missions books, listened to furloughing missionaries report, and given to home and foreign mission offerings. Now some of these senior adults are ready to volunteer. They're past the age of being accepted as full-time career missionaries.

Many opportunities, however, are opening for short-term volunteers who pay part or all of their own expenses. These activities are open for both domestic and world missions. Both home missions in the United States and foreign missions around the world are like different beats of one heart.

Southern Baptist lay people, at the urging of President Jimmy Carter, have gotten excited about a Mission Service Corps to handle five thousand volunteers. For people who don't know where or how they want to serve, a computer service is available. Like a computerized dating service, the system matches up the person and the opportunity. A small fee sent to Volunteer Involvement in Missions, 1350 Spring Street, N. W., Atlanta, Georgia 30309, will bring the information for getting into the computer. An application form for the Mission Service Corps is available from P. O. Box 7203, Atlanta, Georgia 30309.

Many other Christian groups are interested in using volunteers in other parts of the world. Rather than thinking in the older category of "missionary," they prefer the flexible concept of "persons in mission." For instance, Robert Bennett, a lumber executive in California for nearly thirty years, went to Liberia after retirement to aid in Methodist work there. As a skilled pilot, he moved patients, staff, and supplies around remote areas of Liberia.

Harold Crow, after spending twenty-five years as an engineer with General Dynamics, put his experience to work in Liberia, also. At the Ganta United Methodist Mission Center, he reworked and expanded the electrical system to include a leprosarium a half-mile away.

If you are interested in Methodist work, you can write for further information to: Office of Missionary Personnel, Board of Global Ministries, The United Methodist Church, 475 Riverside Drive, Room 1373, New York, New York 10027.

At the same Riverside Drive address is the Service Desk for Volunteers, Commission on Ecumenical Mission and Relations, United Presbyterian Church in the U.S.A.

Other denominational headquarters can supply information about volunteer missions.

Many senior adults were brought up on a glamorized but unrealistic view of missions. They have a vague impression that if they went to Africa or the Fiji Islands, they'd be Billy Grahams and Florence Nightingales. One missionary from Indonesia pooh-poohed the idea. He said, "If you're not a soul winner here, you won't be one over there. Crossing an ocean doesn't make you a missionary."

A retired couple from Asheville, North Carolina, the Hollands, enjoyed sharing their Christian experience with other people in churches around their state. When an opportunity came for them to visit England, they gladly went. They paid their own way. They worked with a British pastor, Alex Steen, who felt a special calling to help Christians share their personal pilgrimage with others.

When Clara Holland's husband died, she felt Satan trying his best to make her give up in defeat and quit talking to people about the faith that meant so much to her. But she found grace and power to continue. Then with Alex Steen and a large group of interested people, she went to Australia and did what she enjoyed. She did the same thing in the Land Down Under that she had done in the Tarheel State—she told people what believing in Christ meant to her life. She is seventy-six years of age and lives by the words of this poem she wrote:

> As I travel here below,
>   And share Jesus as I go,
> I'm not ashamed but glad to tell,
>   How he saved and redeemed my soul from hell.

Do You Qualify?

Beautiful, you say, but I'm not like that woman. Should I consider volunteer missions?

Here are some guidelines to consider. And remember that one person will possess one of these qualities, and another person will have another. Still God can use them all, as different colors of glass put together according to a plan become a magnificent stained-glass window. I think God uses our lives, varied as we are, for his glory.

You love people.   You are interested in people—not just their souls, but in themselves. You want the best for their physical well-being as well as their spiritual well-being. You want to be a friend to people who don't have many friends. You care enough to give the very best— yourself.

You want to get out of a rut.   Miss Lillian, the president's mother, said she got tired of sitting in Plains, Georgia, seeing the same people. She'd been a nurse, a housemother at a college, and the administrator of a nursing home. She wanted something different. She volunteered for the Peace Corps. When my wife and I talked to her in her Pond House in Plains, she said:

"Well, I'm going to tell you right now if you ever had any missionaries in India, I never could find anybody who ever saw one. And I was all over India. Every four months we had a nice vacation, and I went all over India. I inquired of everybody if they had ever heard of a missionary. Nobody had ever heard of a missionary in India. I was the nearest thing to a missionary except one Catholic priest who was home while I was there. In fact, we were told not to ever discuss Christianity, religion, or politics.

"The Hindu man who had been teaching me came to my house after the lady who roomed with me had gone to bed. I wouldn't let any of my Indian friends come till 9:30 because she would slam the door in their faces. He came and wanted me to talk about my religion. I gave him *Good News for Modern Man*. Four months later, he wrote me and said he had read that book—read it four times—and asked if I had a sequel to it."

When Miss Lillian returned from that world-enlarging experience, she was never quite the same. She developed a new respect for people who were seeking God through other religions. Although she had never been a person with racial prejudice, Miss Lillian broadened in her appreciation of each person's worth in the sight of God. She became even more grateful for the advantages of the high standard of living most Americans enjoy. When she returned, she quit eating between meals because she couldn't forget all the hungry people she'd seen in India. (She told Jimmy that even though she couldn't send food to them, she could refrain from wasting it herself.) When she returned to Plains and discovered that her children had built her the Pond House as a surprise, she became grateful every day for its comforts. She told me, "It's just like heaven."

Lillian Carter shared her experience with churches and civic groups and with her family. Her son, Jimmy, has been influenced by her reports. He has made a trip to India himself. The president spoke by videotape to fifteen thousand Southern Baptists meeting in Kansas City, urging them to take a bold thrust forward in volunteer missions. On that occasion, he referred to his mother's experience of studying the languages of India at the age of sixty-eight.

You yearn for adventure.   Admit it. Too often, those of us in our fifties and older think of adventure in the same way we do those roller skates or tennis rackets we played with as teenagers—they served their purpose once but have no utilitarian value now. We discard adventure in the same way.

One woman out in California never had a tennis racket in high school. Peg South didn't start playing until she was sixty-six! Then she went on to win gold medals in the International Senior Olympics. Today, at eighty-five, she is the oldest competitive female tennis player in America. I think it's OK to call her a little old lady in tennis shoes—a term I never use with others because it's such a put-down. But in her case, the shoe fits; and she helps to transform an ugly label to something exciting.

Peg South's same spirit of adventure is a quality that a volunteer missionary needs. It's the same eagerness I detect in touring groups who go around the world, having fun in sightseeing but also meeting missionaries and enjoying these new relationships. These people go back home and tell their friends that the missionaries need a new electric typewriter or a minibus. Their daring has led them to discover the nitty-gritty of missions.

W. C. Ruchti, pastor of the English-speaking Rome Baptist Church, told me that some of his best church workers are youthful American students who have come to Rome to study voice, art, or other subjects. A couple of senior adults could go abroad to study in Rome or Munich or anywhere they learn of an English-speaking church and offer their services. They might not get above-average grades in art classes, but their church work might bring them these remarks someday: "Well done, thou good and faithful servant."

I love the spirit of adventure I saw in a woman's note published in a Presbyterian church newsletter. The eighty-five-year-old writer, Nadine Starr of Lexington, Kentucky, has this qualification of daring that would make her a marvelous volunteer missionary:

If I Had My Life to Live Over

"I would dare to make more mistakes next time. I'd relax. I would limber up. I would be sillier than I have been on this trip. I would take fewer things seriously. I would take more chances. I would take more trips. I would climb mountains.

"You see, I'm one of those people who live sensibly and sanely year after year, day after day. Oh, I've had my moments, and if I had it to do over again, I'd have more of them. Just moments, one after another, instead of living so many years ahead of each day. I've been one of those persons who never goes anywhere without a thermometer, a hot-water bottle, a raincoat, and a parachute. If I had it to do over, I would travel much lighter.

"If I had my life to live over, I would start barefoot earlier in the spring and stay that way later in the fall. I would ride more merry-go-rounds."

You can take disappointments. On the mission fields, the glamor has a way of melting into reality. The gorgeous scenery becomes swallowed up in dust storms. The new converts sometimes backslide. The plans to convert a continent dissolve into long nights of making out budget requests.

A group of volunteer construction workers responded to a mission need they learned about. They went to Brazil to help in a church building project in a remote area that had no church. The local people were supposed to have laid the foundation of the building so that the workers could begin their specialized work as soon as they arrived. They found nothing started.

The Christian workers pitched in, channeling their negative emotions into digging holes and pouring concrete and hammering. Then the building began to emerge, to the surprise of the local people. When the volunteers returned to their churches in the United States, they could bring colored slides of a handsome meeting house, erected for God's glory—an example to the local people of pitching in and doing a task.

Critical people who blame their pastors with worldliness, with being more interested in their families than in the congregation, with thinking too much about money, with putting too much time on study, and so forth will find these same qualities in missionaries. But affirming people who don't expect perfection will find missionaries human and love them for it. And if one missionary evangelist or nurse disappoints them, they won't blame all the other workers. They can take a disappointment without letting it turn their thinking into a stereotype and making them bitter about missions.

One of the pressing needs on mission fields is for dormitory parents at boarding schools that the MKs (missionary kids) have to attend, miles away from their parents. If a woman in her sixties took one of those assignments and expected MKs to be angels, she'd be in for a disappointment. On the other hand, many dorm parents find the children kinder and more appreciative than the average class in the United States; still, there might be an occasional "ornery" type—one to try their patience. Yet these problem children might be the ones, years later, to write that the dorm parent's understanding had kept them from doing something foolish and the older person's influence had headed them in the right direction.

You have special talents. You might claim that you have no talents, but that would be false modesty. God gives his children gifts to use in building up his body, the church. When you take an inventory of skills, you'll find you have one—maybe several. You can actually say you're gifted, talented, or skilled without sounding pompous. Maybe you'd prefer to say that you have certain interests.

Lila Powers of Miami taught English in the public schools there for many years. During that time, refugees from Castro's Cuba came flooding in. She helped hundreds of these people learn to speak and to read English. They were eager and willing to learn. She developed the skill of teaching English as a second language.

I interviewed Mrs. Powers when she visited her son, Bruce, a friend and fellow worker at the Sunday School Board. The retired schoolteacher told me how she had attended the Baptist World Alliance in Stockholm. In that international gathering, someone asked her if she would be willing to teach English in Russia. She was willing, but that opportunity didn't come.

What did develop, sooner than she expected, was an

invitation from the Foreign Mission Board to serve in a place of great need. Within three weeks of her volunteering, she was on her way to Jordan.

On her arrival at Amman, Jordan, Mrs. Powers began to teach English in the Baptist school. After six months she went to Ajloun, where the denomination runs another school and a fifty-bed hospital. The lady from Miami taught Jordanian pastors the English language. She also taught English to the students in the school of nursing. But she used other gifts. She taught piano to the MKs and also to some of the nationals.

Although she had some good language students, she found the Arabs weren't quite as enthusiastic as the Cubans had been. After all, the Cubans needed to learn the language of the land they had immigrated to—just for survival. People in Jordan didn't have such an urgent need, but they still made progress and learned from this spunky little woman from Florida.

Lila Powers saw history in the making. She was in the capital of Jordan when the PLO attempted to take over the government. She saw planes and helicopters moving in to drop troops to the rooftop of the Intercontinental Hotel. She heard cannons roaring and machine guns firing. Still, she didn't feel in danger. She had faith that God would take her safely through that experience. Later she learned that all the missionaries at the compound in Ajloun had been praying for her.

The volunteer missionary witnessed another drama unique to that part of the world. King Hussein was overjoyed when he became the father of a baby boy. The Jordanian king ordered a public sacrifice. Mrs. Powers went to stand in the crowd. A guard took her to the front line, right next to the four camels that were to be sacrificed.

Then she saw the motorcade coming. The king of Saudi Arabia was visiting King Hussein. When the two kings passed the camels, attendants stabbed the four animals. "I was right there where I could see the blood gush from the beautiful camels and watch the sacrifice," said the amazed Mrs. Powers.

Since she has been in the Near East, the retired schoolteacher can understand the world situation much better. She knows something of the turmoil first-hand. She has seen the difficulty of language barriers. She has seen the difference in Eastern and Western customs. She knew their writing is read just the opposite from ours—from right to left. But she didn't know that their hymn music is also written backward (to us). After a lifetime of reading music from left to right, she had to shift gears and read the plaintive, minor key melodies of the East from right to left.

In interviewing Mrs. Powers I told her that when I visited Jordan, a high school student said to me, "I want to go to Hollywood and take up muscle building." These were the two big goals in his life.

She replied, "Everyone I met wanted to come to the United States. Heaven to them is the United States. Many of the refugees who came from Lebanon stayed with us at the hospital compound and, in turn, came to the States." She was concerned that not only the Lebanese pastors but several Jordanian pastors had gone to America. This absence leaves a vacancy in those countries. She is concerned about the scarcity of Christian workers. Many more volunteers could fill places of real need.

Lila Powers assumed no feelings of superiority. She sat with the people in their homes and ate goat meat on rice. She had a genuine love for the people. "The Arabs are very personable people—warmhearted, friendly, kind people. They received me graciously. They've been pictured through the news media as unpredictable, but I found them warm and friendly and helpful and kind—gentle and most appreciative of our work."

I enjoyed my talk with Lila Powers. She's no stained-glass saint; she could talk the horns off a billy goat. But I think she exemplifies several of the characteristics that are needed in a volunteer missionary. She has a basic love of people. She wanted to get out of the sandy rut of Miami living. She, after a trip to Stockholm and Russia, yearned for more adventurous travel. But she knew how to take disappointment. In advance, she faced the idea of separation from her two sons in Nashville and Miami and the grandchildren. In fact, she didn't call them a single time because she thought it would be easier if she didn't hear their voices. She learned the solemn lesson of living alone. "I think loneliness is a state of mind. I have always been happy in my work and happy in whatever leisure time I had; so I have never known the pains of loneliness."

One of her disappointments occurred in her plan to return. She came home on a brief vacation, on the occasion that I met her. She had her return ticket to Jordan. She looked forward to continuing her language study of

Arabic. But the mission board people in Richmond told her she was needed in Rhodesia. I thought that was like jumping from the frying pan into the fire. But Mrs. Powers said, "There's turmoil in Rhodesia, but I have no fear in my heart. The Lord did not give me a spirit of fear. So I am going there with an open mind and a willingness to work where there is a need. We have a large boarding school and a one-hundred-bed hospital in Sanyati, Rhodesia. I love my country, but I also like the challenge of the foreign service. I like the challenge of giving my all without pay. I think the greatest joy has come to me as a volunteer. I was at the top of the salary schedule in Miami. But as a volunteer in my sixties, I perhaps put in longer hours and more preparation for my work than I ever did as a paid teacher. I am getting a much greater joy from it."

So there you have the experience of a person who has tried it out on two continents. She's convinced that volunteer missions is the thing for her. Would it be the direction you need to take? There's one other matter you need to consider.

You feel a divine leadership. There's no reason to think that God limits his calling to pastors. The New Testament teaches that a call comes to every Christian (1 Thess. 2:12). The initial call isn't the final one. God makes his will known. It's not an audible call. He has given you a mind, and he expects you to use it. But the Almighty Creator can work through your feelings and wishes. He can make it known to you if you are called. He doesn't have to resort to skywriting or burning bushes to get his message to you. He can choose any method he wants, but his usual way is to give you some gifts and some thoughts about using those gifts for others.

If you are toying with this idea of God's call, you need to make sure you are experiencing a divine call—not some human pressure put on you by an idealistic writer like me or by a pushy person like your enthusiastic pastor. Some people might even try to use the tool of guilt or obligation on you, trying to make you feel that you must go because *they* think so. That's not a sufficient reason. You should go because *you* think so. You need to be called by God—not by a writer, a pastor, or a neighbor.

You need to go because God has put an interest there— a wish to have fun in this way. The Creator doesn't want you to go out of obligation. He doesn't want you serving as a volunteer missionary just to atone for a guilty conscience; no, there are other ways to make restitution and to gain a sense of absolution. He doesn't want you going because of some emotional pressure that another well-meaning individual has placed on you. That feeling of being directed by another person isn't enough to sustain you when the disappointments begin to pile up.

I believe that God would like for you to volunteer as a short-term missionary if you have the characteristics mentioned earlier: you love people, you want to get out of a rut, you yearn for adventure, you can take disappointments, and you feel a divine call. He'd like for you to become involved in world missions if you want to cook or nurse or farm or teach or keep books or practice medicine or use other talents somewhere in the world for his glory and for your own sense of satisfaction.

Appendix

How well informed are you about your own age group? Here's a simple True-False test to reveal what you really know about aging.

Facts on Aging: A Short Quiz

By Erdman Palmore, Ph.D.

True / False

_____ _____ 1. The majority of old people (past age 65) are senile (i.e., defective memory, disoriented, or demented).

_____ _____ 2. All five senses tend to decline in old age.

_____ _____ 3. Most old people have no interest in or capacity for sexual relations.

_____ _____ 4. Lung capacity tends to decline in old age.

_____ _____ 5. The majority of old people feel miserable most of the time.

_____ _____ 6. Physical strength tends to decline in old age.

_____ _____ 7. At least one-tenth of the aged are living in long-stay institutions (i.e., nursing homes, mental hospitals, homes for the aged, etc.).

_____ _____ 8. Aged drivers have fewer accidents per driver than drivers under age sixty-five.

_____ _____ 9. Most older workers cannot work as effectively as younger workers.

_____ _____ 10. About 80 percent of the aged are healthy enough to carry out their normal activities.

_____ _____ 11. Most old people are set in their ways and unable to change.

_____ _____ 12. Old people usually take longer to learn something new.

_____ _____ 13. It is almost impossible for most old people to learn new things.

_____ _____ 14. The reaction time of most old people tends to be slower than the reaction time of younger people.

_____ _____ 15. In general, most old people are pretty much alike.

_____ _____ 16. The majority of old people are seldom bored.

_____ _____ 17. The majority of old people are socially isolated and lonely.

_____ _____ 18. Older workers have fewer accidents than younger workers.

_____ _____ 19. Over 15 percent of the United States population is now age sixty-five or over.

_____ _____ 20. Most medical practitioners tend to give low priority to the aged.

_____ _____ 21. The majority of older people have incomes below the poverty level (as defined by the federal government).

_____ _____ 22. The majority of old people are working or would like to have some kind of work to do (including housework and volunteer work).

_____ _____ 23. Older people tend to become more religious as they age.

_____ _____ 24. The majority of old people are seldom irritated or angry.

_____ _____ 25. The health and socioeconomic status of older people (compared to younger people) in the year 2000 will probably be about the same as now.

Dr. Palmore is professor of medical sociology and senior fellow at the Center for the Study of Aging and Human Development, Box 3003, Duke University Medical Center, Durham, North Carolina 27710.

To check your score: All odd-numbered items are false; all even-numbered items are true. Take the number you miss and multiply by four; then subtract this number from one hundred. That is your score.

To analyze your mistakes: You can find out how much of an antiage bias you have by counting how many of the following items you missed: 1, 3, 5, 7, 8, 9, 10, 11, 13, 16, 17, 18, 21, 22, 24, and 25.

A Closing Thought by the Author.

A Prayer for Senior Adults

Lord, I'm grateful for the exciting process of aging
   As it takes place in myself and in my friends.
Help them * to grow bold as they grow old.
   Help them know that silence isn't always golden—
   Sometimes it's yellow.

Help them to grow up as they grow old.
   Show them the hidden meanings of maturity.
   Help them to become patterns that others can take
      as models for their lives.

Thanks, Lord, for the excitement of helping others.
   You are purging their souls from boredom, selfishness,
      and pent-up hostility.
   You are giving them a purpose in life, a crusade for
      what they know is right, and a mission to carry out
      the unfinished work of Christ.

Keep them self-affirming,
   But help them to love and to serve others.

                  Through Christ Our Friend and Savior. Amen.

   * If you want to use this prayer with a group of senior adults, change
them and *they* to *us* and *we*.

Notes

CHAPTER 1

1. Words by Henriette Luise von Hayn, 1778; translated by Frederick W. Foster, 1789.
2. Words by Genevieve Lexow, © Copyright 1976 by The Hymn Society of America, Inc. Used by permission.
3. Louis Harris and Associates, Inc. *The Myth and Reality of Aging in America* (Washington: The National Council on the Aging, Inc., 1976). Third printing.

CHAPTER 3

1. Dieter Hessel, ed. *Maggie Kuhn on Aging: A Dialogue* (Philadelphia: The Westminster Press, 1977).

CHAPTER 6

1. Adell J. Harris and Jonathan F. Feinberg, "Television and Aging: Is What You See What You Get?" *The Gerontologist* 17, no. 5 (October 1977), part I, pp. 464–468.

CHAPTER 9

1. Bess Foster Smith, "My Heritage," *Mature Living* (July 1977). Used by permission.